A PARENT'S
BEDSIDE COMPANION

A PARENT'S
BEDSIDE COMPANION
Inspiration for Parents of Young Children

Randolph K. Sanders

HERALD PRESS
Scottdale, Pennsylvania
Waterloo, Ontario

Library of Congress Cataloging-in-Publication Data
Sanders, Randolph K.
    A parent's bedside companion : inspiration for parents of young children /
Randolph K. Sanders.
        p.   cm.
    Includes bibliographical references.
    ISBN 0-8361-3591-1 (alk. paper)
        1. Child rearing—United States.   2. Parent and child—United States.
I. Title.
HQ769.S256   1992
649'.1—dc20   92-4963
                                                                          CIP

A PARENT'S BEDSIDE COMPANION
Copyright © 1992 by Herald Press, Scottdale, Pa. 15683
    Published simultaneously in Canada by Herald Press,
    Waterloo, Ont. N2L 6H7. All rights reserved.
Library of Congress Catalog Number: 92-4963
International Standard Book Number: 0-8361-3591-1
Printed in the United States of America
Book and cover design by Merrill R. Miller

1 2 3 4 5 6 7 8 9 10 98 97 96 95 94 93 92

To
Joy and Alicia

Contents

Preface and Acknowledgments 9

1. Bedtime 13
2. The Child in Your Midst 17
3. Listen 21
4. Going Out in Public 25
5. Share Your Own Experiences 30
6. Time Is of the Essence 34
7. You're in Charge 38
8. Praise: The Painless Discipline 43
9. When Less Is More 49
10. If-Then 54
11. Thank God for Gadgets 58
12. Watch Me 62
13. Self-discipline 67
14. Spanking 71
15. Be Creative 78
16. Finding Old Roots and Making New Ones 82
17. Enter the Inner World 88
18. The Early Evening Battlefield 92
19. Limit Them 96
20. Train Up a Child 99
21. That Kid's Face Looks Familiar 104
22. The Language of Feelings 110
23. Do No Harm 116

24. When the Problems Get Complex 121
25. Silver-Spoon Children 127
26. What Do You Do with an Angry Child? 132
27. "Mommy, Daddy . . . I'm Scared!" 137
28. What Does It Mean to Be Family? 142
29. He Wants Them to Fly! 147
30. Bless Me, Bless My Child 151

Select Bibliography 153
The Author 155

Preface and Acknowledgments

This book is born out of real life. I did not have a perfect childhood and I haven't been the ideal parent.

Fortunately, many fine people have guided and influenced my parenting. Some of them, like my own parents, G. A. and Frances Sanders, have touched my life for years. They grew up in hard times and harsh circumstances. Yet somehow they not only survived but instilled in me a desire to keep growing and learning, a trait that has served well my effort to become a better parent.

Other people, like professors, ministers, and friends, have come into my life for relatively short periods. But they have given me various gifts which have directed my behavior forever after.

My wife, Bette, is my parenting partner. She complements me. She often steps into situations where angels and her husband fear to tread and redeems them. Many times she understands the source of stress in one of our children before I do. She supports me when I'm on the right track and need to stay on it. And she challenges me when all is not well. I hope I do the same for her.

My children have taught me as much as anyone about parenting. Before they came, I had a skeleton of parenting ideas; they added the flesh and blood. I learned much from my oldest, Joy, and new things from my youngest, Alicia. I love and respect them both. I cherish the unique relationships I have with each of them.

—Randolph K. Sanders
New Braunfels, Texas

A PARENT'S
BEDSIDE COMPANION

1. Bedtime

The bedtime ritual is something like the ordeal of a decathlon in the Olympics.

A h, bedtime! Children must love it. Why else would they drag it out from 7:30 until only the good Lord in heaven knows when?

The bedtime ritual is something like the ordeal of a decathlon in the Olympics. The first big event is called *assisting the child in putting on pajamas*. It is similar to sumo wrestling. Parent and child joust until the parent can successfully pin the child long enough to get the pajama pants over both legs. Then comes the second round, in which the parent must successfully guide the child's head and arms through the right openings in the pajama shirt without getting the wrong limb in the wrong hole. All the while the parent must avoid being kicked, jabbed, or pinned to the floor.

Then there's the *brushing of the teeth*. This is one of those places, as the experts say, where the child's drive for independence conflicts with her need for assistance. One night the child insists she can't brush her teeth by herself. You and only you can brush them the right way. The next night she demands that she brush them herself.

Of course, if you leave her alone, the real fun begins. One night I walked past the bathroom. My daughter, I saw, was about to put a toothbrush completely devoid of paste in her mouth.

"Where's the toothpaste?" I asked.

"Right here." She pointed to a microscopic particle of tooth-paste perched precariously on the eighth bristle in the third row.

Some children hate toothpaste. Others seem to adore it. If not watched, these kids would substitute toothpaste for peanut butter. Toothpaste follows them to the sink, the floor, their clothes, and even the toilet seat.

Once toothbrushing and all the other obstacles are out of the way, and the kids are safely tucked in bed, one other hurdle remains. It strikes terror in the heart of any self-respecting mother yearning for her own sleep.

"I need a drink of water."

This request makes parents pull their hair the most. It never occurs right away. It comes only after you've tucked them in, trudged to the living room, slumped down in your most comfortable chair, thought to yourself, "another day done," and breathed a sigh of relief.

This is a book for parents to read after they've delivered that last glass of water and the kids are finally in bed asleep. That's the only time parents have a chance to read anyway.

Parenting young children isn't easy, at bedtime or anytime. Anybody who says it is has no children or never goes home.

Children can nag. "I want to eat at Hamburger Heaven," little Missy says as you drive home from the grocery store.

"No, honey, we're eating dinner at home tonight," you say in what you consider clear and articulate English.

Ten seconds pass. Missy says again, "I want to eat at Hamburger Heaven."

"Didn't she hear me?" you think to yourself. But you repeat your message again, adding that the food at home is more nutritious than the nuggets at Hamburger Heaven. Case closed.

Wrong.

Five seconds pass. Now Missy is speaking in imperatives. "We *have to go* to Hamburger Heaven!"

Children can be fickle. You fix the peanut butter and jelly sandwich just the way they've always liked it. All of a sudden they tell you they won't eat it unless the jelly is confined to one half of the piece of bread and the peanut butter to the other half.

Children can act downright ugly. Recently I overheard three children playing. The two older ones suddenly decided to exclude the younger child and told him to scram.

When the little boy cried, one of the older children turned to the adult nearby and said, "What's wrong with him?"

The woman tried to explain it was because they had excluded him.

The boy said flippantly, "Oh, I thought it was something important," and nonchalantly went back to his game.

Despite such problems, many people end up having children. Most need help at some point in dealing with them.

Unfortunately, letting people know that parenting is a struggle isn't prized in our culture. Most of us, if really honest, are insecure and sensitive about our parenting. The last thing we'd ever want anybody to call us is a *bad* parent. So most of us work overtime protecting our image as good parents even if we're feeling shaky inside.

Consequently, most people keep their parenting problems to themselves. That can be a problem. For one thing, it leaves parents feeling alone and frustrated. They begin to think they are the only ones whoever had such difficult children. This cuts them off from people who could tell them otherwise. Without the feedback of others, and the manual we all thought came with the product, they perpetuate unconscious patterns of parenting that don't work—but are below the level of their awareness.

In a few cases where the child's problems are severe, the parents' need to be seen as "good" parents can lead to serious complications. Sometimes parents send a troubled child to the psychiatric hospital for treatment, only to become upset and anxious themselves when the child improves as a result. It is as if the hospitalization, which helped the child, convinced the parents of their worst fear. Now they know they are incompetent and must rely on others to help them deal with their children.

None of us are perfect parents. Most of us aren't even close. If ever there was a task in life God created to teach us humility, it would have to be parenting. There's no place in this enterprise for supermothers and superfathers. All of us need help. As parents, we are the type of people Jesus of Nazareth spoke of when he said, "It is not those who are healthy who need a physician, but those who are sick" (Mark 2:17, NASB).

This book is for imperfect parents. Forget all your idealistic images from the silver screen and television. Forget "Leave It to Beaver," "Father Knows Best," even "The Cosby Show." You can't become one of those people. They exist only in a scriptwriter's imagination.

I'm not a perfect parent. You aren't either. We won't ever be. But we can become better parents. It's a process of sharing and learning. It starts with frank admission that we all have lots to learn about children. It continues with a willingness to grow day by day. As we grow, we'll become better parents and better people, and our children will reap the dividends.

2. The Child in Your Midst

. . . my children are on loan to me

There she is! My newborn baby daughter! Nestled, gently sleeping, in the crook of her mother's arm. Mother and child are weary from the excruciating task of childbirth that occurred just three hours earlier. Wonderful feelings well up inside me again . . . overwhelming joy, pride, contentment, thankfulness.

In the ancient Greek, there is a word *kairos*. It means "decisive point in time." It is a word used in the New Testament to refer to those miraculous moments when God himself breaks into the daily grind of everyday clock time and does something dynamic—something special (Paynter, 1983). As I look at my newborn baby daughter, I know that with her birth I've shared one of life's kairos moments.

A door slams. My mind is jarred back to the here and now. I've been daydreaming. The picture in the photo album on my lap is of my baby daughter nestled in my wife's arms. But the young girl standing in the doorway to the living room bears little resemblance to the baby in that picture—though their names are the same. Only seven years have passed, but how things change.

The little girl who started life with arms and legs she could barely control—and expressed her needs through tiny cries—now walks to friends' houses, swings from monkey bars, and tells us exactly what she will and won't do. Somewhere in between she learned to roll from back to tummy, walk on two legs, print letters, and add numbers.

Children are a gift from God. But the gift is time limited. For some 18 years, give or take, I have my child. In this time she grows, transforms, and matures.

Carl Sandburg said that

> a baby is God's opinion that life should go on. Never will a time come when the most marvelous recent invention is as marvelous as a newborn baby. The finest of our precision watches, the most supercolossal of our supercargo planes, don't compare with a newborn baby in the number and ingenuity of coils and springs, in the flow and change of chemical solutions, in timing devices and interrelated parts that are irreplaceable. (Sandburg, 1965)

During the first years, a baby develops at a meteoric pace. Consider the first year alone. During the first two months, even before she can do much else, she'll begin to focus her eyes on mobiles you hang above her crib. During the next two months, she'll begin to follow her favorite stuffed animal with her eyes as you pass it across her field of vision. She may even reach out to grab it.

Between four and six months, she'll be reaching out for almost anything of interest and may start to roll over. At six to eight months she may sit up. And between eight and twelve months, she really makes headway—crawling on her tummy where she wants to go, pulling herself to a standing position, and even taking steps with support. That may not seem like a lot if you're with the child every day. But go away for a couple of weeks and you'll wonder if the child you've come back to is the one you left only days earlier.

The first year or so is also crucial to the child's psychological and social development. Erik Erikson (1963) said this is the time when children learn either to trust or mistrust the world around them. Many experts believe the first six weeks are especially crucial to the development of security.

Infants at this age need to feel their parents' loving touch, hear their gentle voices and lullabies, and see their parents' smiles. They need to know that when they cry they can trust someone to answer. That's not to say babies need parents who neurotically grab them up at the slightest whimper. Babies can feel a parent's nervous insecurity too.

What babies do need are parents who will calmly respond to their cries, show them lots of love and affection, and thus communicate that it's going to be okay to live in this world. More than discipline, little babies need parents who will make the house a safe place to explore. Lock up the family heirlooms and the fine china and put safety plugs in the electrical outlets. In that safe haven babies can get into things they should and be kept away from the things that would get them into trouble.

As the child grows, he goes through periods of expansion interspersed with periods of consolidation. During expansion, the child is "stepping out." He wants to explore things and to learn everything he can about anything he can—regardless of whether it is good or bad for him. These are times when his motor skills suddenly get better, or his vocabulary takes a giant leap forward.

On our baby calendar at home, there's a notation that stretches across the fourth week of the twenty-third month of our daughter's life. It reads, "This week Alicia *exploded* with new words and phrases!" Under the entry is a long list of partial words and juxtaposed phrases, all uttered for the first time that week. Alicia was expanding during that period.

During expansion, the child will test you to see how far you'll let him go with all these new things. Sometimes he'll want to see if he can master you in the same way as he has just mastered taking off his shirt, tying his shoe, or going to the potty.

Just as there are periods of expansion, there are also periods of consolidation. During these times, children slow down. They process the things they learned during expansion. Often they are more cheerful and easier for parents to be around. Sometimes they regress, behaving in ways you thought they had outgrown.

Expansion and consolidation are natural phases that continue throughout the growing up years. Children move gradually back and forth between phases as they grow toward adulthood.

And grow they do. One day they will complete this thing we call childhood. They'll leave home and may well start families of their own.

In a way, my children are on loan to me. In the few short years between birth and adulthood, I have been entrusted to start them on the moral, social, academic, personal, and spiritual road to maturity.

It's an awesome task, but a worthy one. It's the one I've been chosen to do. And I'll do it . . . with God's grace.

3. *Listen*

No one can find a full life without feeling understood at least by one person.

—Paul Tournier

As often happens, I came home late from work one summer evening. It had been a hectic day. There was barely enough time to enjoy the last few moments before sundown. I decided to take a leisurely bicycle ride through the neighborhood and invited my three-year-old daughter to go with me. I buckled her into the child carrier on the back of the bicycle and off we went.

It was a beautiful evening. There was a gentle wind in our faces. The last of the sun's orange rays were peeking through the tall pine trees on the side of the road. How could I think of anything save the beauty of this moment?

But I did. We hadn't rounded one block before my thoughts drifted back to work. Had I made all my phone calls? Did I deal appropriately with the last person I saw? Was there something more I could have done?

I vaguely recall that my daughter was talking to me, but I have no idea what it was about. I know I was trying to impress her that

I was listening. At what seemed like suitable times, I threw in an "uh-huh" to assure her she had my attention.

My mind was still at work. The pleasant communion with my daughter had become just an extended work and worry session, albeit in a lovelier setting.

"Daddy?" my daughter asked in a meek voice. There was something about her quiet intonation, the tentativeness in her voice and the question mark at the end of the word "Daddy," that made my ears perk up.

"Daddy, sometimes when you say 'uh-huh' like that," she began slowly, "I get the feeling you're not really listening to me."

Her gentle but piercing statement brought both Dad and bicycle to a sudden halt. I told her I was sorry and certainly listened to her with increased commitment after that.

Listening is one of the greatest gifts we can give our children. It's through listening that I communicate my esteem for my child. Through listening I let her know she can trust me with her deepest thoughts and secrets. Listening seems easy. It isn't. There's a lot more to it than sitting still and staying awake. To listen well, I have to *do* several things.

I listen with interest. I try to assure my child by my physical presence, my attentiveness, my eyes, and my tone of voice that I'm hearing her. I put down the paper and turn my body toward her. I may get on the floor with her so we can be on the same level. Or I may invite her to sit in my lap.

I do my best to withhold judgment. Children tell me reams when I withhold my urge to correct or direct them. When people see me for therapy, they usually share their deepest secrets in a progressive manner. They share some minor failing. Then they watch closely for my reaction. As they learn that they can trust me to withhold judgment, they come to feel they can tell me the deepest secrets of their hearts. Children act in much the same way.

Don't get me wrong. There is a time for parents to make judgments. But not when you are doing the deep listening I'm talking about here. Deep listening requires care. Listening to your child's deepest thoughts and feelings is like being in a museum full of rare urns, each perched atop a pedestal. One false move and you knock something over you can't replace with the change you've got in your wallet. Likewise, when listening you want to be careful with the secret treasures your child has entrusted you with.

When listening deeply, I want to hear my child's feelings. Feelings are a powerful part of our psyche, for good and for evil. Because they are so powerful, we fear and tend to deny them. We tell people we aren't angry when we are and that we aren't sad even when we feel like crying. We even convince our minds we don't have certain feelings—though the rest of our body may give us away when we come down with an ulcer or some other physical malady as a result of the pent-up feelings.

Sometimes our behavior betrays our true feelings. Take Kevin. He was tough and big for a nine-year-old, and often in trouble. He and his younger brothers lived with his grandparents. Kevin's mother had died suddenly in a tragic accident. His father had a chronic mental disturbance and had nearly abandoned the family.

If any child had a right to feel grief and anger, it was this one. Yet when asked about these feelings, he insisted he had none. In fact, he presented a believable case for his wellness—until he gave himself away. For the more he talked about being in fine shape, the more his jaw became set. He spoke through clenched teeth. His whole body became rigid in the chair. His face got red. Finally big tears streamed down his face. All the while he insisted he had everything under control.

Our feelings, and those of our children, are real and we deny them at our own risk. When we can learn to identify our feelings, and help our children identify theirs, we give those feelings a name. Then the feelings have less power over us. When we deny feelings like anger or hurt, they become mysterious seething caldrons that lurk below the level of conscious awareness yet still wreak havoc. Once we've named our feelings our head finally gets some control over our heart.

So when we listen to our children and help them identify their feelings, we give them a great gift. I hear an angry tone and say, with no judgment, "It sounds like you feel angry . . . tell me about it." Or I see tears and say with real empathy, "Talk to Daddy about how you feel." Such comments help a child name feelings, express them appropriately, and thus gain power over them.

You can start to listen long before your child has begun to engage you in so-called meaningful conversation. I remember when my daughter Alicia was just beginning to try to talk a lot. Perhaps one word in five seemed intelligible to me.

One morning I decided to sit down in her play space and train my ear to listen to her. I reasoned that if I turned my entire hearing and even my visual capacities in her direction, I might understand more of what she was trying to say.

As soon as she knew she had my attention, she started talking with abandon. Much of what I heard was still baby gibberish, but I kept letting her know with my eyes, smiles, and voice that I was doing my best to listen. Slowly, here and there, another word or two became intelligible. Some of her personal vocabulary, words that young children make up to fit some object they don't quite know yet, also began to make sense. I learned that morning that "fa-fa" was Alicia's word for waffle.

The nicest thing I learned came at the end of my listening session. Alicia slowly grew tired of talking and began to turn her attention to other things. But before she did, she looked at me and smiled. She said in words that were easy to decipher, "I wuv you, Daddy!" Even the smallest child loves to be listened to!

4. *Going Out in Public*

Parenting in public is like putting on a play
for an audience . . .

Somebody with a pitchfork, horns, and a red suit invented the modern supermarket. We've been seduced into believing that the grocery store is the place where, in air-conditioned comfort, we can meet all our basic hunger and thirst needs. In reality, the supermarket is a place where parents are tempted toward insanity.

Some agency of the federal government should force stores to place warning signs at the entrance to some aisle. Take the aisle where the children's breakfast cereals are. Here countless varieties of cereals with cartoon characters on the front stretch for 50 yards or more along the bottom shelf, within easy reach of any two-year-old. Each box carries some large print assuring that lots of Vitamin X, Y, and Z have been added to each box. Yet we all know every brand has one major ingredient in common— sugar.

Then there's that rack at the entrance to the check-out lane. At adult eye-level are those scandal sheets. "ROCK STAR ADMITS BEING RAISED BY WOLF PACK 'TIL AGE TWO!" While they've got you distracted reading the paper, your kids are busy rifling through all the chewing gum, candy, and Taiwanese toys tantalizingly placed along the bottom rack.

You really didn't plan to buy raspberry-flavored bubble gum in the shape of Goodyear tires. But it's a little tough to put it back once junior has unwrapped the package, stuffed two pieces in his mouth, and chunked what's left on top of the scanner which mechanically calls out the name and price—before you can give the clerk your regular excuse about your son just having been adopted from a war-torn country where all he had to live on was the chewing gum given by passing soldiers.

Most of us want our children to behave well in public. For one thing, we don't want them to make us look like deadhead parents in front of other people. But we also want them to behave well in public because that's simply something they need to learn.

But being out in public is hard for children. There are so many distractions, so many things for them to pay attention to besides us. In addition, some public places, such as nice restaurants and church sanctuaries, are designed more for adults than for children.

When we try to guide our children in public, we are confronted with one big obstacle. Everything we do to guide them and everything they do in response occurs in the public eye. If we're out at the Megamall and Sissy acts up, everyone sees. That can be threatening to parents. We become tense and defensive. Whether we're conscious of it or not, we worry about how we appear to others. This affects the way we parent at the time.

We often don't realize that our children are affected by being in the public eye too. They may thus react differently than they would at home. They may act up more in public, especially if, when they have misbehaved in the past, we have given them what they want to appease them.

They may assert their independence more, feeling in themselves the freeing quality many public places give. Christine was unsure of herself before riding the mini roller coaster at the theme park. But afterward she was proud of herself. Out of that pride soon grew a haughtiness that led her to run ahead of her family and almost get lost on the way to the next ride.

When corrected in public, children sometimes feel the need to rebel all the more, as if they were putting on a show for the gathering public. Parenting in public is like putting on a play for an audience. Unfortunately, like good actors most children and their parents feel they must play their lines with more drama and flare when they have an audience. Both sides must show the audience they are in control.

Most parents will have the experience of asking junior nicely to put the box of Sicky Sweet Cereal back on the grocery shelf. At home he would do a task like this with little prodding. At the store, he collapses on the grocery floor as if shot, writhing and gnashing his teeth, making his parents look as if they failed parenting school.

Dealing with children's misbehavior in public isn't easy. It can be done, however. And it must be done if children are to develop healthy social selves.

My prayer when my children and I leave the house for the outside world is that I will parent their misbehavior with wisdom and good judgment. I want to do so despite the distractions and awkwardness that arise when parenting in the public "fishbowl."

At least two things help me do this. When misbehavior occurs, I look for ways to cut down on the audience. As mentioned before, dealing with a child's misbehavior in front of other people almost always creates stress for parent and child. And stress almost always leads parent and child to react poorly.

Consequently, when significant misbehavior occurs, I look for ways to get out of the public eye. Once my wife and I had to go on a business trip together. We left our daughters with relatives. As many parents know, children sometimes act out more soon after their parents return from an extended absence.

It didn't take ours long. When we arrived at the airport, we met our children, then went to a nearby cafeteria for lunch. We had hardly gotten into the serving line when one of our daughters started testing us.

"Why can't I have that dessert?" she asked. Her requests quickly turned to demands. Before we knew it, she was whining, one step from throwing a fall-on-the-floor, kick-and-scream tantrum. Though it was inconvenient, I told my wife what to get for me, picked up my daughter, and headed for the front door. Once outside, I felt pressure lift, that pressure we parents always feel when with a hysterical child in a public place.

We went straight for the car. There we sat until she calmed down. As the crying subsided, I told my daughter in a clear voice that once she had calmed herself, stopped crying, and decided to quietly eat with the rest of us, she could rejoin the family.

At first she started crying again. But I repeated my demand firmly. I added that we would not leave the car until she had done what I asked. Soon, in the quiet of the car, away from the tension of the restaurant, she regained her composure. We walked hand in hand back to the restaurant.

Even better than dealing with problem situations when they happen is anticipating them and preventing them from happening in the first place. It doesn't take long to identify the places where your children tend to act up the most. It could be a particular place, such as the toy store. At toy stores even normal children sometimes go bonkers from the overstimulation of having so many toys gathered in one small place.

It could be with certain people. I knew a little girl who was the picture of mild manners. But when with one friend, she suddenly became a hellion. Somehow the two became a wrecking crew when together.

Whether it is in a particular place or with particular people, anticipating potential trouble spots can help you guide your child into healthier behavior. Children can learn to control behavior, especially if they know what you expect from them ahead of time. During one particularly miserable outing at J. C. Penney's, one of our daughters discovered what she considered a wonderful activity. She would run away through the racks of hanging clothes brushing each garment with her hand as she went by, then run from her parents when they finally found her.

The next time we went to Penney's, we sat down and had a talk before we left the house.

Dad: We're getting ready to go to Penney's.
Child: (Child jumps up and down, jubilantly)
Dad: Settle down a minute. We're going to go to Penney's but I'm concerned about something. The last time we went, you ran away from us and knocked dresses off the rack. That upset me. I don't want it to happen this time. This time I want you to stay with me. I want you to ask me before touching anything. Do you understand what I want you to do?
Child: Yes. . . . But, Dad, can I look at the shoes?
Dad: Yes, if I'm there with you and if you ask me before touching any of them. Do you understand?
Child: Yes.

That trip to Penney's went much better. Now, before we go to a mall, a restaurant, a grocery store, or other public place, we sometimes talk about the expectations we have for our children's behavior. Many times, it helps!

5. Share Your Own Experiences

Let me remember the hard places of my own youth,
so that I may help when I see him struggling—
as I struggled then.

—Angelo Patri

Childhood can be a painful time. We adults forget all too quickly how painful it can be. When I was a child, adults always told me how easy a child's life was. I could never figure out where these adults grew up. It wasn't in my neighborhood.

Had they forgotten what it was like to be laughed at because you were too skinny, too fat, or just the wrong shape? Had they never suffered the embarrassment of being tripped and knocked to the ground by the class bully while their best friend watched? I figured the adults in my life must have contracted amnesia in their twenty-first year.

Now that I'm an adult myself, I realize why grown-ups think the child's life is easy. Adults have to pay the bills at the end of the month. They have to decide between difficult options. They have to be mature enough to lead a family. To an adult, playing in the sandbox looks like pretty simple stuff.

But that's looking through an adult's eyes. If I were a child, just starting out in life, the things that seem easy now would be tough. I wasn't confident about reading aloud in first grade, thus criticism of my reading hurt me a lot more then than it would now.

And some of the things we adults consider so easy wouldn't turn out to be if we had to do them now. It's just that they don't happen anymore. I don't have many bullies trying to pick a fight or knock me down anymore.

Our children often get the wrong impression of us. They think we don't understand what they're going through. They complain about the school bus ride being loud and tedious. Instead of identifying with them, we challenge them to a game of "I Had It Harder Than You."

You know the game. It's the one where we tell them that riding the bus is nothing compared with what we had to do when we were their age. "Why, when I was your age. . . ." Our stories make us feel smug, but they fail to impress our children.

We should share our growing up experiences with our children. But we must do it in the right way. We should share things that will edify our children. We should communicate so our children know we understand what they're going through. To do that, we need to think about our memories as we did when we were children.

I realize some childhood experiences are so painful it is hard to find anything edifying in them. I know some adults who were abused as children. They not only find little to share with their own children, they may be totally unable to remember anything about certain years in their young life.

Many of us, however, can remember things that happened to us. If we allow ourselves to remember them through the eyes of a child, even some painful experiences can help our children.

When one of our daughters was approaching her sixth birthday, she made a list of people she wanted to invite to her party.

Because she was going to have the party at a water park, she could invite only a limited number of guests. For several days, she struggled to come up with just five names. During her deliberations, she mentioned several times that she might want to invite Josh, her "boyfriend" from school.

When the day came to turn in her list, Josh's name was mysteriously absent. "I thought you were thinking about inviting Josh to your party." I said.

She turned her face away, lay down on the sofa, and put a couch pillow over her face. The muffled voice from under the pillow said sheepishly, "I don't think I want to invite him now."

She was embarrassed and self-conscious about liking a boy and wanting him at her party. My heart was touched. Her feelings struck a nerve in my own past.

"I remember something kinda like that happening to me once," I told her.

She took the pillow off her face and sat up, fixing her eyes on me. "You do?" she asked.

"Yes," I replied. "I was in kindergarten and it was Halloween time. Because we lived in a place where there weren't many houses nearby, my mother offered to take me in the car to trick-or-treat at a few of my friends' houses.

"There was a little girl in my class named Debra. I sure did like her. I remember one time we even sat on the steps outside the school together. I really wanted to ask my mom to put Debra's house on the list of places to trick-or-treat, but as the time got closer, I started having funny feelings. I felt a little embarrassed and told Mom I wasn't sure I really wanted to stop at Debra's.

"Mom was real nice though. She told me she would go up to Debra's door with me if I wanted; that made me feel better. On Halloween, when we got to Debra's house, I still felt a little nervous, but I went to the door anyway. And you know what? Everything came out okay. Afterward I felt sort of glad I had done it."

Later I was in the living room working when I overhead my daughter talking to her mother. "Mom," she said. "You know

I've already made out my list of who to invite for my party. But I was thinking. If one of those children can't come, do you think we could invite Josh?"

My daughter understood herself just a little better that day and gained some confidence in the process. I like to think I helped.

And by the way . . . Josh did come to the party.

6. Time Is of the Essence

Parenting takes time . . .

I've had it with the concept of "quality time." You know, it's the concept that you really don't have to spend *that much* time with your children so long as it's truly *quality time.*

Now don't misunderstand me. Balancing time between children and the rest of life is important. Parents who believe it is their solemn duty to spend every waking and some not-so-awake moments with their children are in for trouble. Any stranded homemaker can attest to the depression that sets in when one tries to make parenting a marathon endurance contest.

Children don't get your best under such circumstances. What they get is a burned-out, crabby shell of a parent. They get a parent irritated by their every word, who lacks the creativity to deal with their childishness, and wishes their kid would turn twenty-one in the next twenty-four hours.

But I also worry about children who don't have enough time with their parents. Every time I see Barbara Walters interview another Hollywood star about his family life, and he talks about having great quality time with his kids sandwiched between shooting on location in London, Cape Town, and Tokyo, I think about children like Jake.

Jake's dad was a professional entertainer who traveled the country. He never could stop playing long enough to pay attention to his family. When Jake's mother had enough, she divorced him. Jake spent most of his time in private boarding school. Jake idolized his father, though he had been with him all of three times during the year.

Jake's father probably thought those were quality visits. Once they went to Disneyland. Another time they went deep-sea fishing. Later in the year they went to Colorado for a ski trip.

If you had asked Jake, he would have said they were quality visits, too. Jake kept a little corner table in his room where the mementos of these trips with his father were displayed, like shrines to a distant god.

But Jake was in trouble. He regularly got into fights with other boys at school. He was lazy about getting his homework in. Though he could hardly carry a tune, he used to tell everyone who would listen that he was going to be a musician just like his father.

Jake was sent to a therapist when his grades got so bad he was about to be permanently expelled from school. The therapist worked with Jake for the next few months. Jake made great progress. Everyone shouted the therapist's praises. He had worked a miracle with the boy!

It would be nice to say that Jake's miraculous improvement was due to some elegant therapeutic technique. Actually, Jake improved most when his therapist started taking the time to play Ping-Pong with him in the clinic rec room. During those times they'd play a round of Ping-Pong. In between they'd sit and talk.

No magical psychoanalysis was performed. No trip to Disneyland. Just some Ping-Pong and some really good talks. They were the kind of talks boys like to have with an older, wiser man—talks about getting along with other people and having self-confidence. They were the kind of talks parents have with children—talks that take time and require good timing.

If you're going to make quality time more than a cliche, you must have more time available than you think you really need.

Young children don't interact on schedule. They haven't learned about clocks and deadlines. The thirty minutes you sandwiched in to play with your son may be almost gone before any real play or communication begins.

When I was working in one particularly demanding job, I found more and more of my family time being devoured by work. I was kept late into the evenings by counselees with serious problems and community concerns that demanded my attention.

One of my solutions was to draw a figurative wall around Saturday mornings. These mornings were to be spent with my family—not just thirty minutes or an hour but the entire morning.

I focused my attention completely on the children. We played, rode bikes, or did chores together (chores done together are family time well spent too).

Sometimes things wouldn't develop quickly, but since I had arranged plenty of time, they didn't have to. Most important, since there was more time, there was more chance to intersperse good talks in between whatever else we were doing. Talking with children often works best when the two of you are involved in some activity. Communication can then emerge as a natural byproduct.

Drawing on the little chalkboard at home can lead naturally to a talk about the fight that happened at the chalkboard at day-care earlier that day. Playing with dolls in the dollhouse can lead to talk about how the dolls treat each other—and how real people treat each other. Even some television shows, when watched together, can be communication starters.

Parenting takes time, lots of it. A century ago most people lived on the farm. Quality time could be interspersed with the day's work, since families were together most of the day anyway. Now Dad goes in one direction to work, Mom goes another, and the children go to day-care or school.

Despite the fact that the quality of our lives is better now than in the last century, it's doubtful the quality of our time with our children has improved much. In fact, our driven culture makes us think we can spend less time with our children as long as we are efficient about it.

That might be true of assembly line work, but it's not true of parenting. Parenting will always take time. It's time we adjusted our goals and priorities to reflect that fact. It may mean making less money. Or saying "no" to the next move up the corporate ladder even though no one in the company will understand why you have "chosen to sacrifice your career." It may mean one less committee or one less service project no matter how honorable the cause. It may mean putting off some personal goal until the children are older.

I realize some families can't do this. For them, working extra hours is not a luxury but a necessity. But these families often do a better job of providing quality time because they are acutely aware of how crucial it is. In their scraping and scratching for survival, they bind together as a family in work. They savor their time of play like rare morsels of fine chocolate.

Most of us could afford to live with a little less though, especially if it meant improving relationships with our children. Living in simplicity is not a virtue in this culture anymore—but it should be. Few children in the world have as many material things as our children do. But our children also grow up with a frightening sense of entitlement such as the world has seldom known. They've had things and they have an insatiable thirst for more.

Perhaps what they really need are fewer things and more of you and me. Real quality time and lots of it is a kind of living water. It quenches the thirst of children for the things that really matter in this life: intimacy, fellowship, and love.

7. You're in Charge

Children are by definition, immature. If they were otherwise, they would not be children.

Once upon a time a spaceship carrying two small aliens from another planet made an emergency landing in a cow pasture somewhere in America. Unharmed, the aliens made their way past some bewildered cows until they came to a rather typical American farmhouse inhabited by a rather typical American couple.

The husband and wife were understandably shaken when they found two space beings hanging around on their front porch. But they quickly adapted to their new guests and took them into their home with little reservation.

After all, the aliens were quite attractive. They were diminutive, about three feet tall. They had pleasant little cherubic faces. Their skin was soft and their hair fine and silky. They had tiny hands and feet. At times they seemed cuddly and dependent.

The farm couple felt honored and awed to have these cute little space creatures in their home. As people often do in such circumstances, they went out of their way to give their guests everything they wanted.

Over time it became clear, at least to the couple's friends, that no matter how cute they were, these aliens were not superior to earthlings. At least they weren't superior emotionally. They had just enough understanding to get themselves into lots of trouble. They lacked good judgment and common sense. For instance, they loved the water—but couldn't understand why they couldn't jump into the deep end right away.

When the couple tried to tell the little earth invaders not to go into the water until they learned to swim, they became stubborn. They whined that it wasn't fair they should be denied the pleasures of the water when all around them earth creatures were frolicking freely.

At first the husband and wife tried to placate the little beings. They did everything they could short of placing the creatures in obvious danger. After all, the creatures were special guests.

The more they tried to appease them, however, the more stubborn the little guests became. The couple started having second thoughts about whether sheltering aliens was such a good idea.

Finally the couple began to lose control of their own emotions. One neighbor reported that she saw the farmer's wife in the hardware store carrying on a heated argument with the space creature over whether he could have a chain saw for Christmas. The neighbor reported seeing the wife violently shake the space creature. The space creature screamed and threatened that if he didn't get the chain saw, he would report her to the SPCA (Society for the Prevention of Cruelty to Aliens).

The neighbors were dumbfounded by all this. It was clear the farm couple was bigger, and, potentially at least, more mature than the little space bullies. Yet it seemed these pint-sized aliens were winning the battle of wits.

Why didn't the farmer's wife just stop yelling, pick her little charge up, and remove him from the hardware store? Why didn't she just refuse to come back until the little guy had learned how people on this planet act when they go into a store?

But then why can't we parents do this with our young children? Why do we get ourselves into purposeless shouting matches that go nowhere?

Sometimes it's because we're like the farm couple. We make the mistake of assuming that because children can be cute, charming, cuddly, and loving, they are also mature. They aren't.

As wonderful, as intelligent, as beautiful as children can be, they can never be more than children. Children are not miniature adults. They are immature because that's what children are. Children, aside from being neat and warm, are stubborn, selfish, and sometimes downright rude.

We parents make a big mistake when we assume our special little child won't be like all the rest. Ours will be well-mannered and generous, friendly and courteous—an adult disguised in a cute face and Osh-Kosh overalls. Any fantasies we have that our child will be extraordinary are usually dashed between the eighteenth and the twenty-fourth month when the terrible twos begin. At that point we either get terribly discouraged, decide to try again by having another baby, or face the truth.

And the truth is that children are, by definition, immature. Immature means that sometimes they'll be rude, stubborn, and surly. Should we just accept these behaviors? NO!

What we can do is face these behaviors in the same way a good teacher faces a child who hasn't yet learned to write. We realize we have a skill to teach this child. It will take time, repetition, consistency, and above all, a lot of love.

It makes no sense to fantasize that a child will suddenly know how to write when she's had limited experience with letters, pens, and pencils. Likewise, when my child is being rude and unruly, it makes little sense for me to think, "Why can't she just act right?" when "acting right" means acting like an adult. She can't act like an adult because she hasn't learned how to be an adult.

That's where I come in. I'll help her learn how to be a person who can use good judgment. I'll help her to learn good manners, to set and work toward goals, to cope with not always getting what she wants.

I've got time to teach her these things and I will. I'll take charge. Some days will be frustrating. As in school, there will be lots of repetition. I'll hear myself trying in many different ways to instill concepts we will have been over many times before.

Some days she'll act fully grown at age five. Other days she'll act like a two-year-old when she's eight. But I'll keep working with her.

Sometimes I'll be tempted to say, "You know better than to do that." But I'll try not to assume she knows better until I'm absolutely sure she does.

Some days I'll feel like giving up or giving in. Most parents do. This parenting isn't easy. But as a parent, I'm the one in charge. And I'll own that responsibility. In some families, it's very unclear who the people in charge are. Chaos reigns.

We were eating at a cafeteria when our table began to shake and rattle. Knowing earthquakes are not common in Texas, I suspected something else was causing the commotion. The next thing I knew, a little boy of about four, dressed in his best suit, boots and a bow tie, came crawling out from underneath the tablecloth.

Ignoring me, he crawled over to the next table where he repeated the same act to those diners' dismay. The next time we saw him he was running around the restaurant with a clear plastic cake cover on his head. He looked like a boy ready to go on a space mission in his Sunday clothes. He had somehow managed to take the cover from one of the desserts in the cafeteria serving line. We looked in vain for anyone who might be his parents. The one family that looked like he might belong to them walked out without him. There was no one clearly in charge.

In our family, I want it to be clear who the people in charge are. I certainly don't mean this in a rigid, dictatorial sense. I'm no middle-aged bully out to throw my weight around and show my children who's boss.

In fact, if your main goal in being in charge is to show your children who's boss, to be the high potentate of some underaged serfs, you're missing the point. What being the authority for authority's sake will get you is a lot of needless power struggles with your children.

Take choosing the clothes your child will wear each morning. At around age two or three, many children get very particular about what they will wear. You could march in each morning, lay out a set of clothes for them, and demand that they put them on or else. You could then have your children take you on in a fight for the right to wear a purple instead of a blue shirt.

Or you could decide to avoid the power struggle. You could lay out two or three outfits, all of which are agreeable to you, and allow the child to pick out the one she wants. In this way you remain the final authority as to suitability, color, and so forth. But you also give your child the chance to learn how to make a good decision on her own.

When we started doing this in our own home, I was surprised to see how quickly Joy learned how to pick colors that matched. She apparently learned this by seeing the selections we gave her to choose from each day.

Being in charge means being clearly aware that my wife and I are the designated parents. As such, we are the leaders. But good, secure leaders allow freedom to those in their charge so the younger generation can grow up healthy and ready to take charge themselves someday. As a parent, I want to provide firm but flexible parameters within which my children can grow and become the unique people they were created to be.

8. *Praise: The Painless Discipline*

Catch'em Being Good

—K. Daniel O'Leary and Marlene Schneider

Eighteen-month-old Jimmy just took his first, random bite of cooked carrots. I saw him moving his hand in that direction and started watching him out of the corner of my eye. As soon as I could see that he had the carrots in his mouth long enough to taste them, I turned full in his direction and gave him a big smile. I laughed and exclaimed, "All right! Carrots!"

Jimmy looked back at me, smiled contentedly, and went right on munching his carrots. He turned next to his mashed potatoes and my attention shifted to other things. But later, when he reached for some more carrot, I was ready again. "That's a good eating boy!" I exclaimed with another big smile as he smilingly chewed up another piece.

At the end of the meal, Jimmy had ice cream. It was clear he liked it. There was no need and no good reason to encourage him to eat it. So I concentrated on my own ice cream and the conversation with my dinner host and hostess.

I was helping Jimmy to like carrots. I was doing it without pain or pressure. Judging by the initial results, if someone keeps up the training program, Jimmy may come to like a healthy food that lots of youngsters think they are supposed to hate.

Simple praise was what made the difference with Jimmy. I let him know, by giving him positive attention at the moment he tasted the carrots, that I was pleased with what he was doing.

Praise is one of the best, most pleasant, least painful forms of discipline anybody has discovered. Praise as a form of discipline? Well, remember that discipline is all about teaching. And praise certainly qualifies as one of the world's great teaching tools.

To paraphrase a fundamental law of learning psychology: things that receive praise tend to be repeated. If Jimmy is praised for eating carrots, it increases the chance that he'll eat his carrots next time.

Maybe you're thinking, "Why call this discipline, since Jimmy wasn't engaging in negative behavior? He wasn't refusing his carrots or spitting them out."

But that's precisely why praise is such a wonderful form of discipline. By giving Jimmy praise at the outset, I helped him and me avoid the potential for lots of negative behavior. And in child rearing anything positive is better than the negative.

There are many forms of praise. Some are direct, like telling the child something you like about what he is doing. Many are indirect, like simply turning your attention toward the child when he's doing what you want. Research has shown that children will increase behaviors, whether good or bad, that parents, teachers, and other important people attend to.

When can you praise?

You can praise when your child is playing appropriately with others.

You can praise when your child has just shared one of his toys.

You can praise when your child has just made amends for something he/she did wrong.

Reading this, some of you are probably ready to put the book down. You already know praise is important, helps children learn, and builds their self-esteem.

Why read further? Because there are important rules you need to know if praise is going to work for you.

If you use these rules your child will grow. You'll enjoy each other a great deal more. Without these rules, your praise won't be effective. You'll mistakenly assume that while it's a nice ideal, praise will never work in your house.

Rule 1—Don't wait too long to praise a behavior you want your child to continue. If Andy just colored within the lines of his coloring book, tell him now. Don't wait until next week. Above all, don't praise him for coloring within the lines if he's drawing on the walls at that moment. He won't get the right message.

Rule 2—Don't praise indiscriminately. A few years ago some researchers (Hart, Reynolds, Baer, Brawley, & Harris, 1968) decided to test the theory that children are troubled because they don't get enough praise and attention. They asked some teachers to give praise and attention to a troubled, antisocial preschool girl no matter what her behavior was. They hoped the little girl would be overwhelmed with all this positive adoration and improve her behavior. Nothing happened. She remained as difficult as always.

Then the researchers told the teachers to limit their praise, giving it only at times when the girl was actually cooperating with other children. The amount of time the little girl spent playing pleasantly with other children increased significantly, from 2 percent of her day to 40 percent.

Not just praise makes the difference in a child's life—but praise given for the right things. Don't praise your child when she's being disruptive. Do praise when she does something right.

Rule 3—Look for things to praise your children about. Most of us are trained to look for problems that need solving rather than good things that need praising. We're a fix-it culture. Search for the things your child is doing that deserve praise, then give her some. She'll spend more of her time doing those positive things and will be less likely to get involved in problem behaviors.

Admittedly, trying to do this can be a problem for parents with especially difficult children. These children spend so much time getting into trouble, they seldom seem to do anything praiseworthy. Actually they do, at least sometimes. Unfortunately, their parents get so overwhelmed trying to stay in control of the children's negative behavior, they understandably fail to notice things the children are doing right. When the fatigued parents see little Broomhilda playing quietly with paper dolls, they lay low, take a break, and just pray this calm in the storm will continue.

But that's the very time they must let Hilda know how pleased they are with what she's doing. Doing this regularly will make a big difference in Hilda's behavior. If you want the good behavior to continue, you've got to catch the child doing it, then let the child know about it.

Rule 4—When you praise a child, be specific. Don't just tell Bruno he's a good boy. Tell him exactly what it was he did that you liked. "Bruno, it's fantastic, the way you're sharing your colors with your sister," you say as you pass by his room.

Rule 5—All children like praise. But some get self-conscious with lots of vocal praise. Others get uncomfortable if you praise them in front of other children. *With these kids, make your praise less obvious.* Use fewer words. Praise just by spending extra time with them. Say nice things to them when their friends aren't in the room. Whisper positive comments to them that others can't hear.

Rule 6—Praise the child based on level of improvement. An example will illustrate this rule. Should you praise your second-grader if she just brought home a D? The answer is—it depends. If her previous grade was a C, the answer is no. If her previous grade was an F, the answer is yes.

"Ah," you say, "but A's and B's are the only acceptable grades in my house." I'm sorry to disappoint you, but if you refuse to praise a second-grader when she's making improvement, whatever the level of improvement, she'll become frustrated. She'll give up, and you'll never see the A's and B's you desire.

Start where your child is and build from there. Praise for small increments in improvement, rather than require that the child obtain the final goal before praise is given. Most parents know how to do this instinctively when the child is just learning to walk. They start by praising the child for trying to stand, then for standing supported by the coffee table, then for walking with support. The same principle applies to other things.

Rule 7—If you want to praise a child who has been behaving poorly, wait until after the poor behavior has stopped, and more positive behavior has begun. When one of my daughters was having a tantrum, I left the scene, telling her I would return only when she calmed down. After a few minutes, her screams stopped. I peeked in. She was quietly looking at a book on the floor. I went in and told her how pleased I was that she had been able to calm herself down and find a book to look at. I also offered to spend a little time looking at the book with her. She readily accepted.

Now that you know these seven rules, you also need to know about a couple of things that are *not* praise. Sometimes when parents get exasperated they use these techniques hoping they'll work. They don't. They have the effect of encouraging bad rather than good behavior.

Succumbing to a child's coercion is one mistake. Igor's been acting up at the store. You say that if he'll just shut up, you'll be forever grateful. What's more, you'll buy him an ice-cream cone.

It seems to work. Igor will be quiet to get the ice cream. But in the process, he'll also learn that next time he goes to the store, the best way to get ice cream is to scream at the top of his lungs until his father gives in. In effect, you praised him not for shutting up, but for screaming in the middle of the store.

Coaxing is also *not* praise. It may be filled with flowery language but it is not praise. "Oh, *please* be a nice girl and eat your prunes for Mommy. You'll be such a sweet girl if you do, and you'll make Mommy so happy. Now you want Mommy to be happy, don't you?" Mommy will be lucky if she gets to square one with this approach.

In coaxing, the parent is pleading with the child. In effect she surrenders her role as parent and subjugates herself to the child. The message the child gets is, "My mother feels inept and without the confidence to lead me and parent me. She is, without knowing it, placing me in control of whether or not I eat my prunes. Not only that, she's placing me in charge of her happiness." That's a pretty strong position for a child to be in and one most children won't resist. They'll refuse to eat their prunes and watch Mommy shrivel in the process.

Children rarely think consciously about wresting control from their parents. But when given the opportunity to take the upper hand, most children are too immature to resist the temptation.

Praise, when used in the right way, is a powerful teaching tool. What's more, it fosters intimacy, closeness, and pleasant memories in a way few other things can. I've forgotten lots of things that happened when I was a child. Praise memories stay with me.

One of my early preschool memories is of an aunt who had a beautiful smile which she delighted in sharing with me and the things I was doing. I'll not forget the day my first-grade teacher hugged me and told me how proud she was of me for finishing my school work despite being out sick for several weeks. And I remember my first baseball coach, who praised me for everything I did right and encouraged me past everything I did wrong.

Praise works. And it feels good too!

9. *When Less Is More*

*Sometimes the best discipline will mean less,
not more.*

I was sitting at the dining table busily doing the family paper-work. My four-year-old slumped into the chair across from me.

"Daddy, can I go out in the backyard and play with Linda?" she asked.

"Sure," I said, assuming that would end the matter.

She remained slumped in her chair. A pregnant pause followed. Then rather casually she said, "Daddy, get my shoes for me."

"No, I'm not getting your shoes for you," I replied, just as casually. To make sure she understood I added, "It's okay if you go outside, but you'll have to get your shoes yourself."

She whined, "You *have* to get my shoes!" Then she began a re-frain. "I want my shoes, go get my shoes, I want them now!"

I paused in my work just long enough to think, "What do I do now?" I could ignore her. But what was my patience level? Could I take the whining?

Deciding to ignore her, I turned back to my work. The intensi-ty, shrillness, and persistence of her whining increased. I buried myself in my work.

The next time I noticed her, she was lying face down on the couch, yelling into the sofa cushion that she had to have her shoes.

I continued my work. After a time (I don't know how long because I really *was* ignoring her), I noticed out of the corner of one eye that she was getting up and slinking off toward her room. She left without a word. A few minutes later, I caught sight of her walking quietly toward the back door. Her shoes were on her feet.

In graduate school, they would have called what I did "extinguishing maladaptive behavior." In lay language, it boils down to ignoring rotten behavior until it goes away. I actually did very little. I just sat there. But in this case doing less meant more in terms of the effect it had on my child.

Ignoring is especially helpful with whining episodes and temper tantrums. It's a great way to get these behaviors to go away without resorting to lots of my own unpleasant behaviors.

Ignoring poor behavior does work. But two rules must be followed. These rules cannot be broken under any circumstances.

First, *the ignoring of the bad behavior must be absolute.* No one can praise or encourage the bad behavior, or even attend to it in any way. If anyone does attend to it, it won't go away. It will get worse. For this reason, I seldom use ignoring when other people are around unless I already know that they too will completely ignore the child.

Suppose you and your wife ignore your son's wacky behavior at the dinner table. But your daughter always giggles at him under her breath. Then ignoring will *not* work.

Occasionally parents and grandparents conflict over ignoring behavior. Some child behaviors grandparents think are cute, aren't so cute to Mom and Dad. That's because Grandma and Grandpa don't have to live with Grandchild everyday. Grandpa may think it's cute to see two-year-old Wendy ooze oatmeal out her mouth onto the floor. But he wouldn't like it if he had to clean it up everyday for the next week.

Often grandparents can be enlisted to help ignore the behavior. If Grandpa laughs at Wendy's oozing, tell him privately that you've been working on a plan to help her stop. Tell him why you don't want her oozing. Perhaps you think he should know this already. But remember it's been a long time since Grandpa had to clean one of these messes himself.

Explain to him gently that cleaning up this goo off the floor is driving you crazy. Explain how ignoring works and enlist his aid in making it work. If Grandpa suggests some other technique, express your appreciation—but tell him you want to give this plan a fair trial first.

The second rule for effective ignoring is this. *Use ignoring only if you have the stamina and patience to put up with the bad behavior until it is exhausted.* In my example, you'll notice I asked myself, "Can I take this whining?" It's an important question.

Ignoring behavior works eventually, but it is likely that the bad behavior will actually get a little worse before it gets better. Children don't give up easily. If I use ignoring, I must be willing to accept this. Suppose just once, during the episode with my daughter, I had gotten fed up and yelled, "Stop whining!" or had started trying to calm her down. Then I would have encouraged rather than discouraged her bad behavior.

I must decide in each situation whether I'm up to the task. If I'm not, I had better use another method of discipline.

Ignoring the behavior is not the only "less is more" discipline. Another is called "time out." Time out means removing the problem child from a setting that is encouraging him to keep acting up. It means putting him in a setting where there is no encouragement for his behavior.

Take three-year-old Monica. She was using the sofa as a trampoline. Despite a warning to stop, Monica kept on, smiling and giggling, daring anyone to spoil her fun. Mom went over, grabbed her little darling in mid-jump, and put her in a small chair in the corner of the hallway. There Monica sat alone for two minutes. If she left the chair for any reason, she would be placed back until she completed her two minutes.

That's time out. Monica's mom took her out of a setting that was encouraging her to keep acting up—the couch and an audience. She placed her instead in a lonely setting where none of the encouragers were available.

Time out, of course, isn't a new concept. People have been sent to the corner for years. In the past though, time out has often been thought of mostly as punishment. Actually time out can be a positive disciplinary tool. Its fundamental purpose is to remove the child from a situation that's encouraging poor behavior so the poor behavior can extinguish.

Think of it as a variation on ignoring. Indeed, time out is often helpful when ignoring isn't possible or hasn't worked. Rather than continue ignoring a child that won't be ignored, remove the child to a solitary place where his behavior can truly be ignored.

Time out usually does not have to last long to be effective. Most parents are tempted to make it longer than it needs to be. Young children rarely need much over five minutes. Remember that little children have different time concepts than we do. Two minutes may seem an eternity to a three-year-old.

In fact, instead of emphasizing a certain length of time in the chair, you might like to make time out an opportunity for the child to regain composure and make her own choice to improve her behavior. This is especially good when the child is agitated.

Instead of setting a time limit, tell the child that when he has calmed down and feels ready, he may leave time out. Then he may come to you and talk about what happened. Now, if indeed he has calmed down, you can briefly explain why you put him in time out and what you expect from him now. You can ask him to repeat what you've said so you can be sure he has understood and is ready to offer more positive behavior.

If a number of minutes have passed and the child hasn't come to you, check on her unobtrusively. When you notice she seems to have calmed down, go to her and calmly ask if she's ready to talk about what happened. Most often she will be and has just been reluctant to take the first step.

Whatever the specific method of time out, make sure the child understands what he must do to end it. Whether you require a set time in time out or not, you will probably want the child to exhibit a minimum of acceptable behavior to end time out.

If so, tell him that at the outset. Then if junior has come to the end of a three-minute time out and is still having a screaming fit, remind him that to end the time out he must stop the screaming. Tell him you're going to set the kitchen timer for another minute and you'll check his behavior at the end of this time.

Time out is nice for a number of reasons. It gets the child out of a situation in which he's likely to keep getting in trouble. It keeps him from getting attention for poor behavior. It allows him a quiet place to cool down and use his own wits to think about his behavior and more positive alternatives.

The parent too can benefit from time out. By putting the child in an isolated spot away from your immediate vicinity, you'll be more likely to stay in better control of your emotions. Then you'll be more objective and effective with the child.

By now you probably realize that while ignoring and time out may require *less* rather than *more* observable intervention on your part, they require no less commitment. Ignoring requires a commitment to fully ignore until the child's behavior has stopped.

Time out requires that you make a time out place available for your child. That you follow through and use it when necessary. And that when you use it, you follow-up afterward to make sure the child has learned in time out whatever he needed to learn.

10. *If–Then*

Misbehavior has its consequences.

Life is made more secure because some things we do are followed rather predictably by certain consequences.

If I do my job, *then* I get my paycheck.
If I stop going to work, *then* I will lose my job.
If I drive like a maniac, *then* I'm likely to have a wreck.
If I take drugs, *then* I'm likely to get addicted.
If I eat right, *then* I'll be healthier.

Life is full of *if-then* statements which express the basic truth that actions do have natural consequences. Some actions typically lead to positive consequences. Some lead to negative ones.

I realize actions do not *always* lead to the expected consequences. Sometimes incompetent workers get big paychecks. Reckless drivers may escape without a scratch while safe motorists get hurt. In the great sifter of life, though, the basic if-then truths tend to fall into the bowl more often than the exceptions.

That's good. Life would be pretty chaotic and unpredictable otherwise. It also encourages us to learn to be responsible. If my actions lead to certain consequences, some positive and some negative, I should learn which actions lead to which consequences.

It's important for children to learn about the consequences of their actions too. We parents are the designated teachers. To be sure, we can protect our children from learning these lessons if we want to. We may say we are protecting them out of love. But we really aren't doing them any favors.

There was a granddad raising his grandson because the boy's parents had been killed in an accident. It was a tragic loss for everyone. Granddad was trying to do right by the boy. He had good intentions. But because he felt so sorry for his grandson, he thought he would do the boy a favor by protecting him from the consequences of anything he did wrong.

When the boy wouldn't eat his dinner, he excused it because he understood that the boy's appetite might be poor. When the boy used his fist to flatten another boy down the street, Gramps chalked it up to all the frustration the boy had gone through. When he started getting in trouble at school, Grandpa went to the administrators in his defense, trying to make sure the school understood what a hard life his grandson had had. By the time the grandson was a teenager, Grandpa had a tyrant on his hands—a young boy on a collision course with the juvenile probation office.

Grandpa deserved an A+ for understanding his grandson's anger. What he failed to realize was that no tragedies excused his grandson from learning a law of the universe: his behaviors would have consequences. Now the state would have to teach him.

If you want your children to learn that logical consequences follow their positive and negative acts, start now. Children as young as three or four can benefit. In fact, children this age often respond remarkably well to such discipline.

One day my four-year-old spilled her milk all over the linoleum floor. In my mind I was screaming. How could she inconvenience me like this? Didn't she know I had lots of things to do that day? I wanted to blame and scold.

Then I remembered the "if-then" formula. With some trepidation, because I wasn't sure she would respond positively, I said, "Okay, *if* you spill your milk, *then* you gotta clean it up."

To my surprise, she responded without a hint of resistance. "Okay, Daddy. Gimme da paper towas." And with that, we got down on the floor and went to work. We had to do it together. I could not expect her to do a first-class job by herself.

Sure it took time. But it takes time to yell, spank, then clean up the mess yourself. And the best part of if-then discipline is seeing your child walk away from what could have been a self-denigrating experience feeling good about herself. As my daughter finished the job, the look on her face told me she felt proud of herself for being big enough to help clean her own mess.

If-then can be used with a variety of problems. Here are examples. Leshanda goes into a neighbor's house without permission. She may not go into any neighbor's house for the rest of the day.

Gabe throws a tantrum. In the process he breaks the new pen his father gave him. Gabe's father refuses to buy him a new one but tells Gabe he can earn the money to buy himself a new pen.

Sandra refuses to eat any of her seafood supper because "fish is gross." She won't eat any of her side dishes either, even though she likes them, because she "hates the fish." Sandra's parents explain that supper is served only once a night. They warn matter-of-factly that if she chooses not to eat, she'll receive no food, snacks, or dessert until the next meal (breakfast). When Sandra still refuses her meal, the parents follow through.

In each of these situations, I have implied that the parent is responsible for making sure the child experiences the consequences of his actions. In some situations, nature itself will provide the consequence. When I was a toddler and put my hand on a hot waffle iron while my mother's back was turned, I learned in that one lesson that hot waffle irons were nothing to play with. I needed no spanking or even scolding to learn the lesson.

Let me quickly add that letting children experience the consequences of nature should never be an excuse for parental neglect. Brenda was playing close to a hot space heater. Instead of intervening, her father decided to leave her alone. He reasoned that if she touched the heater, it would teach her not to do it again.

It's true that touching the heater will teach Brenda not to get so close again, but the price of the lesson is too high. Purposefully leaving a young child in potential danger is not good discipline. It is harmful neglect. The only lesson neglected children learn is that parents cannot be trusted to keep them out of danger.

If-then should not be used when other methods of discipline would be more helpful and less harmful. Quinn was doing poorly in second grade. His mother chose to allow Quinn to suffer the consequences of his poor work by getting an F if deserved. But waiting until the semester is over for Quinn to "learn his lesson" is much too long. It will probably do no more than discourage Quinn even further. It would be more effective for Quinn's mother first to try tutoring and praise for small improvements in Quinn's work as a way of helping him bring up his grades.

When the if-then formula is used, parents need to make sure consequences they provide for the misbehavior are *logical* for that behavior. David broke a toy that belonged to his best friend. His father refused to let David play with his friend for a week. The problem here is that the father's action doesn't really make sense as a natural consequence of David's mistake. The "discipline" doesn't fit the "crime." Having David replace the broken item would be an appropriate consequence.

The if-then formula works best when three conditions are met. First, the child's problem behavior is fairly clear-cut (spilling milk). Second, the child has the ability to help rectify the problem (the child can use paper towels). Third, the parent sets a consequence that follows naturally from the child's problem behavior (cleaning up is the logical thing to do after one spills milk).

The if-then formula is not for every situation. It is another of the many good forms of discipline which, used wisely, can help children learn about the natural consequences of life as well as how responsibly to fix their own mistakes.

11. *Thank God for Gadgets*

They're good helpers.

Thank God for all those little things that help make us better parents.

Little things, by definition, are those gadgets that help us with the parenting process. One of the simplest, yet most profound, is the adhesive sticker.

You can buy them in rolls for pennies a piece. They come with all kinds of cartoon characters and artwork on them. Young children love them.

When one of our girls was two-years-old, she decided she was too old to ride in her car safety seat. I'd approach the car to put her in and she'd start resisting. She would arch her back and flail her arms, making it hard for me even to get her through the car door, much less in the seat.

Bending over with my upper body stuck inside a hot car in the middle of summer, forcing a child into a car seat, has never been my idea of a good time. My discomfort encouraged me to do some creative thinking about how to improve this ordeal.

My wife, Bette, had bought a page of miscellaneous stickers. Some had pictures of kittens on them, some puppies, and others cartoon characters or flowers and butterflies.

The next time we walked out to the car, I told my daughter we were going to start a new game. Each time she got into her car seat cooperatively, she could earn one sticker. We would put it on a chart on the back of the seat in front of her.

I showed her the page of stickers and asked which she'd like to get that day. She pointed to the kitten. I encouraged her to get into her seat. She did without a hitch. I buckled her in, let her pull off the kitten sticker, then stuck it on the chart in front of her.

Each time we went somewhere in the car after that, we followed that procedure. I always made sure she was buckled up before she selected her sticker. After a couple of times, my daughter had forgotten all about defying me. She was now absorbed in trying to collect as big a collage of stickers as she could.

The gadgets we use in parenting have different purposes. Some are *encouragers*. Encouragers are things that help children do something we want them to learn to do. I wanted my daughter to learn to get into the child seat without incident. The sticker *encouraged* her to change her behavior.

Some gadgets function as *signals*. Signals are things that help remind children of something.

Kitchen timers are a fine signal. The one we have has probably kept a lot more children on track than it has kept pot roasts from burning.

Suppose you want to help your five-year-old get ready for bed. He always falls into this whining blue funk as soon as you mention getting his pajamas on. Instead of abruptly telling him to stop whatever he's doing and get ready for bed, tell him you're going to set the kitchen timer for eight minutes. Tell him he can use this time to finish up whatever he's playing with now. At the end of the eight minutes, it's going to be time to put on pajamas and get ready for bed.

Our kitchen timer has a big dial on it. It ticks like an old clock, which is nice because the ticking serves as a continuous reminder to the child that the timer *is* on and the bell *will* ring soon.

The timer can help children make the transition from one thing (playing) to the next (going to bed). They also help us avoid getting into power conflicts over time with our children.

Little posters and signs can also function as excellent signals in a variety of situations. For the child who keeps splashing water out of the bathtub, draw a red stop sign with a picture of a child splashing water on it. The sign could be hung over the bathtub. Every time the child sees it, or every time you point to it, it will function as a novel reminder not to splash water.

Gadgets are more likely to work if you follow three simple rules. Always be positive when introducing a gadget. Focus on the novel aspects of the gadget. Tell the child how it will help her but don't focus on the misbehaviors that may have led up to your decision to use the gadget.

Be consistent in using the gadget until it's clear that the child can do well without it. A good way to find out if it's needed anymore is to gradually withdraw using it. Test to see if the child continues the desired behavior. There's no need to tell the child you are withdrawing the gadget. Just don't use it occasionally and see what happens. If the child asks to have the gadget back, it's probably not time to take it away yet.

At some interval after the child has learned to do well without the gadget, praise her. You don't have to remind her the gadget helped or that she's doing well without it. Just tell her how much you like the thing that she's doing.

Having said all this, one other thing is important to remember. Some gadgets are effective but not necessarily good for the child. Television, for instance, can be a good gadget for both education and entertainment. But when parents don't monitor shows, or when it's used to excess, it is not a good gadget. It may become a substandard babysitter which makes the parents' day easier but hurts the child.

What makes a gadget good? It should be humane. Things that

demean children are not good no matter how effective. A good gadget does not abuse the child either physically or psychological-ly. Good gadgets make you a better parent. It's true they may also make your parenting task a little easier—but that is not always true, and it must never be the primary reason for their use.

Good gadgets are an accessory to a child's betterment. The gadget by itself won't make a good parent but can help. Wearing a wristwatch won't guarantee you'll get to all your appointments on time either—but it is certainly an effective accessory. Gadgets likewise are good helpers.

12. *Watch Me*

Children have more need of models than of critics.

—Joseph Joubert

The hands on grandmother's new cuckoo clock were positioned at ten in the morning. As the clock chimed ten beats, three-year-old Jan and her mother raced toward the living room. Mom hoisted Jan up to the clock, exclaiming, "Look, the cuckoo clock, the cuckoo clock!"

Just then tiny dancers came twirling out of the trap door on the front of the clock. The little music box inside filled the air with the sounds of "Edelweis." Jan laughed and clapped her hands.

At eleven, the clock chimed again. Again mother and child raced to the living room. Again Mom lifted Jan toward the clock in time to see the dancers do their thing. At 11:30, Mom left for a brief trip to the grocery store and left Jan with Grandmother.

At noon the clock chimed. Footsteps raced toward the living room. It was Jan all right, but this time she bounded into the living room laughing and carrying her doll under one arm. As she approached the clock on the wall above her, she quickly hoisted her doll high above her head in the direction of the clock and exclaimed, "Look, Dolly, the cuckoo clock, the cuckoo clock!"

Children learn by example! They watch how we act and whether we know it or not, they copy us. They also watch how we respond to stress. They look at our moods. They see how we care for our things. They observe what we spend money on, whom we keep as friends, and how we treat our spouse.

Most often, they fashion their behavior directly from ours. Occasionally, if our model is a negative one, their behavior may be a reaction to ours (Krumboltz & Krumboltz, 1972). Barry was a shy, quiet child who never seemed to get angry about anything. When he was about eight, Barry's parents squabbled with a delivery man who had brought the wrong chair. Admittedly there had been a mistake, but even Barry could tell some clerk in shipping, not the delivery man, was to blame.

Still Barry's parents stood in the front yard screaming obscenities at the delivery man while Barry had to stand next to them and watch. Other people down the block started looking out their windows. Barry had never been so embarrassed. He vowed that day that he would never allow himself to get that angry. Not only that, he promised himself he would always be quiet and learn to accept things the way they were.

Whether children imitate their parents' example directly or they behave in reaction to it like Barry did, the example set by parents is important. Yet of all the ways we teach children, our example is often the one we are least aware of.

My friend Jim is the son of a minister. As he was growing up, he listened to at least a few sermons on honesty. His father may remember them. Jim does not.

Jim does remember the time his father took Jim and several of his young friends to a drive-in movie as a special treat. They drove up to the ticket booth and Jim's father paid for their tickets. As they edged away from the booth toward the viewing area, Jim's dad recognized that the attendant had returned too much change.

With no hesitation, Jim's dad turned the car and went back to the ticket booth to return the extra money. The dismayed man at the booth could hardly believe what was happening. Thanking

Jim's father, he told him that in the many years he had worked the booth, it was the first time anyone had ever returned extra money.

Jim was never more proud of his father than at that moment. That one little episode has remained etched in Jim's own system of values right into middle-age. Interestingly, when Jim, himself a minister now, spoke about this incident in a sermon of his own, his father had absolutely no memory of it.

Your example will have a powerful effect on your children even though you may often not be aware of the model you are setting. That's why lots of parents feel frustrated, helpless, and guilty when I talk about the importance of setting a good example. They would like to improve their model, but they aren't sure what their model is. And they certainly aren't sure how to improve it.

I don't want to encourage guilt. If you feel too guilty, you'll just get depressed. That won't make you a better example. Also when people feel guilty long enough, they get frustrated about how hopeless they feel. Then they may look for someone to get angry at or blame. And the target usually ends up being the child.

What I'd like you to do is to take whatever guilt you feel and let it motivate you to become a better model for your children. The way you become a better model is by becoming a better person yourself. As you help yourself, you help your child.

Thus effective parenting isn't just an exercise in caring for someone smaller and weaker than yourself. To be really effective, it means improving yourself as well.

To be a better example, you have to overcome the myth that you cannot change. You can. You won't do it overnight and you'll never be perfect. But you can do better.

First take an inventory of yourself. Find the places where you are the model parent and the places where you fall flat on your face. Stand back and observe yourself as your children see you. If you were them, what would you look like to them? Be honest with yourself, even if it hurts. If you can't be honest with yourself, bite the bullet. Ask your spouse how you look.

Larry asked his wife to help him identify his problem areas. The first thing she mentioned was how sensitive he was to criticism. Even truly harmless teasing usually threw Larry into a tailspin. As the couple talked, Larry realized that both of his children were sensitive too. Probably they were learning this from him.

After you've identified your problem areas, make a plan for improving one of them. Pick only one, because you are going to need to stay as conscious as you can of what you are modeling in this area.

Larry watched for the times when his wife and children teased him. He began teasing back in a fun-loving, nonthreatening way.

At first this worked well. But then he found that his teasing took on a biting quality. What had started as harmless bantering had become a cold war.

Larry began to look to his own childhood for answers to the question of why teasing seemed to hurt him so much more than it did others. He suddenly realized that as a child his older brother had teased him mercilessly. In his mind, his parents had done little to stop it. He had taken his resentment with him into adult life. Now when anyone teased him, even his children, he became defensive and rude.

Larry sat down with his wife and shared with her the roots of his problem with teasing. Together they worked out a plan. He would tell her when he felt hurt by her teasing. She would reassure him that she meant nothing rejecting by it.

In the process, their children saw a father learn how to be less sensitive. They then learned how to be stronger themselves. As a bonus, they learned moms and dads can improve, or at least cope better with problems in themselves.

It's no secret that improving yourself, thus improving the example you set for your children, is not easy. Sometimes professional counseling can help. Often people who come to see me for psychotherapy are motivated partly by worry of what their behavior is saying to their children. When I work with the parent of a young child, I almost always see improvement in the child and in the parent-child relationship as a result of the parent's courageous choice to seek counseling.

Children learn by our example. Knowing this, we can put away our pride, examine ourselves, and grow personally. As we do, we can know that since our children are taking in everything we do, they will undoubtedly gain in the process.

13. *Self-discipline*

From self-control comes freedom . . .

—Richard J. Foster

It was one of those sandbox conversations. Four-year-old Alicia and I were preparing sand-cakes with wild berry topping. While we mixed our culinary creations, the conversation turned to bad words.

"Daddy," Alicia inquired. "Are some words bad words?"

"Yes, honey, some words are bad words," I replied.

Brief pause. "Now, Daddy, don't get mad at me, okay?"

I knew she was about to name a No-No word. She wanted to make sure I understood she was just naming the word, not using it. "Okay," I replied.

"Daddy, is 'stupid' a bad word?"

"Some people use the word stupid, but we don't call each other stupid," I replied.

"Sometimes when I get really mad at Joy, I call her that word," she explained.

"I know. Sometimes when you get really mad, you feel like saying those things. But a better thing to do is to tell your mind to say, 'I'M MAD AT YOU, I'M ANGRY AT YOU, or I'M UPSET WITH YOU,' when you get mad at Joy."

"Yeah, but sometimes part of my mind takes a vacation, Daddy. This part," she said pointing to the left side of her head, "stays here, but the other part goes on vacation."

We paused a few minutes to take our sand-cakes to the imaginary oven by the swing set. Then we went indoors to eat lunch.

At the table Alicia said, "You know, Daddy, I think I'll tell *that* part of my mind to take a vacation."

"Which part, Alicia?"

"The part that wants to call other people bad names. I'll tell that part to take a vacation, then I won't call people a bad word."

Alicia didn't know it, but she was disciplining herself. For the young child, learning self-discipline involves two basic steps. First, the child has to take the disciplinary messages other people give her and internalize them. She has to get them into her head in a way that's understandable to her. Rather than hearing her mother's audible voice tell her to keep away from the hot stove, she has to hear a voice from within saying, "Danger, get your hand away from the hot stove!"

After she has heard this inaudible command from inside, she has to take the second step. She has to obey the voice and act accordingly. She has to keep her palm off the stove.

Even toddlers can learn to discipline themselves. It isn't uncommon to see a little one, barely able to talk, self-disciplining. Once I saw a little girl tempted by the forbidden stereo in the corner of the family's living room. The colored lights on the panel and all the shiny, silver knobs were quite tempting.

But each time she approached the console, she stopped just short, looked at the stereo, then at her outstretched hand. Quickly she swatted her outstretched left hand with her right, back-peddling from the stereo and saying, "No, do not touch!"

Do you want to teach your young child some self-discipline? Remember the two basic steps. She must internalize the disciplinary messages you and others give her. And she must act on them.

One way to help her do this is to teach her to "talk to herself." She doesn't have to do it aloud, though in the case of the two-year-old approaching the stereo, it probably works better that way. But as children get older, they can talk to themselves internally, under their breath, and thus control their behavior.

One of my girls came home one day having learned a new way to "win enemies and influence other people." Kick them in the shins. This behavior, both Mom and Dad agreed, needed to be banished from her repertoire.

In addition to other disciplinary measures, one of the things my wife, Bette, did was to teach our daughter how to talk to herself about the problem. With our daughter in the bedroom, Bette began demonstrating. "When you're getting mad at someone and you feel yourself wanting to kick them," she explained, extending her foot in a kicking gesture, "tell your foot, 'Foot, don't kick!' " While demonstrating, Bette shook her finger at her foot for a little extra pedagogical emphasis.

If you use a teaching method like this with your child, you might even have your child practice with you. Have her extend her own foot then stop herself as she tells herself not to kick. You could also teach her to express her anger in words as an alternative to using her feet. "When I feel my foot wanting to kick, I'll remember to use my words and say, 'I'm mad at you,' instead."

Sometimes you can help your children figure out their own internal messages for controlling impulses. Just ask your child, "When you're telling yourself to kick somebody, what could you say to yourself instead? What could you say in your mind that would stop you from kicking and make you do something else?"

Children are surprisingly able to find their own novel ways to exert self-control. One day my wife and I were in the garage adding water to the car battery. Our four-year-old was watching. I wasn't watching her as I left the battery, with its caps off, to get a rag from the trunk.

"Now, whatever you do, do not touch the battery or those caps," I warned.

"I know, Daddy. See my hands?"

I looked at her for the first time. She had her arms crossed and had tucked each hand tightly under the opposite armpit. I realized she had already practiced some self-talk. She had told her hands where to go to stay out of trouble. She was keeping them there. She was practicing self-discipline.

Someday your children will grow up. When they do, they will no longer have you around to discipline them. The one primary discipline that will remain with them, even into adulthood, will be the self-discipline they have learned. To the extent that they learn it now, they will be able to practice it then. The power to discipline oneself enables one to live more uprightly. But it also enables one to live with greater freedom and self-confidence, secure in the knowledge that one has internalized basic rules for living that will protect one from harm's way.

14. *Spanking*

*. . . I'm going to ask you to look at what we know
about spanking, both the good news and the bad.*

Spanking is a sensitive topic. People don't just think about
spanking. They feel about it. There's enough haggling, controversy, and fiery oratory to fill volumes.

I'm not interested in more controversy. The adversarial posture we have adopted about corporal punishment, the "for it or
against it" mentality, has prevented us from seeing the truth.

I want to be heard as respecting the views of those who oppose
spanking. I particularly appreciate the dilemma of parents whose
peace church traditions tell them violence is wrong. How can they
use the implicit "violence" of a slap and simultaneously train the
child in the way of peace? All of us, including me, need to think
carefully about this.

Hoping not to polarize you one way or the other, let me ask
you to look at what we know about spanking, both good news and
bad. I'm going to tell you I think spanking has a place in discipline.
But I'll warn you to be very careful with it.

First, let's look at what we know. Spanking helps control children's behavior. Most children will stop a behavior when spanked

for it. Many will cease and desist with the mere threat of a spanking. Spanking works.

Second, most Americans do spank their children, at least occasionally (Rubin & Fisher, 1982). Often we develop fantasies about what other civilized people do that simply aren't accurate. We imagine ourselves to be the only parent in the country who ever whacked his kid on the rear. We guess Model Mother next door and Reverend Monkhouse down the street would never do such a thing. Yet probably both of them have. If you spank your children occasionally, you aren't alone.

Don't get me wrong. The fact that a majority apply their hand or something else to their child's bottom does not make it right. Over the centuries, majorities have supported all kinds of things that haven't been right.

But most Americans do spank, at least once in a while. And many of the children of these parents will turn out fine. What's more, one could make a case that some parents who don't spank probably should. These parents spend incessant amounts of time browbeating their children verbally. They control them with cruel threats to self-esteem and other verbal jabs which serve as an alternative to spanking.

Others lay horrendous guilt trips on their kids, shaming them into submission. Such parents might actually save themselves and their children a lot of grief if they stopped the verbal put-downs and administered quick but humane corporal punishment.

But now that I've said spanking is effective, most people do spank occasionally, and some people who don't spank probably should, I should add this. Spanking is not a necessity for good parenting. There are plenty of adults who were never spanked by their parents and have grown up to be good citizens.

Children who aren't spanked aren't necessarily spoiled or delinquent. They aren't, that is, if they have received other types of discipline which have done the job. Limit setting, time-out, and the other types of discipline mentioned in this book are all good. For many children, they will be enough.

We should also realize that spanking, if overused or wrongly used, can instill an attitude of anger or rebelliousness in the child. The Bible says it well. "Do not provoke your children to anger; but bring them up in the discipline and instruction of the Lord" (Ephesians 6:4, NASV).

Some spanking "provokes children to anger." Such children may appear contrite to the parent who does the spanking. But they act out their growing anger toward younger siblings, peers, and even other adults. Over time they mask a passive resentment that will eventually become full rebellion.

Spanking can have an even darker side. It can become child abuse. To make matters worse, many people who abuse their children don't make a good distinction between what is permissible corporal punishment and what is abuse. They deny their abuse much like alcoholics deny that they have a drinking problem.

It's frightening to think that there are adults who don't have a trustworthy internal warning light telling them when they are going too far with their dependent children. That's why we must be extremely careful in allowing light corporal punishment. It explains why we must set careful standards for its use.

The first is that spanking should be used sparingly. It should never be the main disciplinary technique. Like a strong medicine, the prescription on spanking should read "for very occasional use only."

Pediatrician Wayne Grant (1983), speaks of spanking as the heavy artillery of parenting. It should never be used when a "pop gun" approach will do. If you use spanking for every minor infraction of the rules, what will you do when your child acts out in some major way?

Spanking is a useful final adjunct to other forms of good discipline. It is useful as an alternative when other forms have failed. When used in this way, it's helpful if parents have some formula in their head for how many other forms of discipline they will try before spanking is used.

This tends to make spanking a natural part of a stepwise process of discipline. The parent might start by warning the child. If that didn't work, the parent might use time-out. If that still wasn't effective, the parent might *then*, and only then, use spanking.

Following a set pattern keeps the parents from turning to spanking in an impulsive moment of anger. It also helps them feel free to go ahead with spanking at the proper preset time rather than waiting until they have lost patience and lost control of the disciplinary process.

An immediate spank may be useful in situations where the child's inappropriate behavior will benefit most from a discipline that is quick, sure, and lets the child know Mom and Dad are very serious about the problem issue at hand.

When two-year-old Wendy is just about to find out what it feels like to touch the hot stove, a firm "No!" coupled with a quick swat on her buttock may be what she needs to help her learn hot stoves are not for touching.

We've said spanking should be used sparingly. But how should you spank? Before you ever spank your child, sit down and commit to memory the set method by which you will spank. Most experts recommend that you use the flat of your hand across the buttocks. How hard? Just hard enough. Never so hard as to leave bruises or injure in any way. Just hard enough to lightly yet clearly make the point. If you must go farther to make the point, stop. It's time to get help to find out what's going wrong.

How many times should you swat? Once or twice is plenty.

Internalizing such rules right now will help insure that even though you may be upset when you spank, you will follow the same sane approach to spanking each time.

Many parenting books suggest that you never spank in anger. That's great if you can do it. Most parents I know are angry when they spank. What helps most is to have the clear set of rules for spanking firmly in mind. When you have made a commitment to yourself to limit yourself to two spanks with an open hand no matter what the circumstances, you are less likely to let the anger of the moment overcome you.

Let's be clear. Being angry at your children when you spank is one thing. Being enraged is another. If you are in a fit of rage when you spank, stop. Take a long walk.

Think about what happens when parents spank while in a rage. For one thing, the child rarely makes the needed connection between the misbehavior and the spanking. If you ask such a child later what the spanking was for, she will not be able to tell you. What she will remember is the giant (that's what we look like to them), standing over her with a beet red face and eyes bulging from the sockets, threatening to whip her to within an inch of her life.

When the parent's rage is so severe or the spanking so intense that the child loses sight of what they are being corrected for, the spanking is no longer discipline. It's harsh punishment. It's more about hurting than teaching the child.

Parents who spank in rage also teach their children that out of control behavior and outright aggression are permissible ways of settling problems. It's difficult for children to learn self-control if they see supposedly mature adults going bananas with rage. We must never forget that our children are always learning from the example we set, even the example we set while spanking them.

Avoid spanking children in public when possible. Spanking is an exercise in discipline, not public humiliation. Take children to a back room if need be. If they are old enough, tell them their behavior has earned them one swat a soon as they get home, but don't put them or you on public display.

Babies should *never* be spanked. They have no idea what you are trying to communicate when you spank them. If your baby is on the changing table and wiggling while you try to change him, don't spank him. Just find a better way to hold him in place so you can diaper him.

Somewhere around the time children start walking, spanking can usually be added sparingly to the disciplinary repertoire. Then as the years go by, nature and common sense dictate that you rely less and less on spanking and more and more on other types of discipline.

Now let's suppose you've spanked your child and you have followed all the rules. One thing remains to be done. That is a time of reconciliation. A spanking is a stressful moment, for both parent and child. That's why a spanking is never complete until parent and child get together afterward.

After Melody calmed down from her spanking, her Dad came in, picked her up, and held her in his arms. "I love you," he said quietly and lovingly, "but I don't want you running out in the street ever again. It scares me because children can get hit by cars and hurt badly when they run out in the street. Do you understand what it is that I don't want you to do?"

Reconciliation time assures your child that the spanking is not rejection. The parent still loves her. It's also a time for the parent to review with the child the reason for the spanking.

When a spanking doesn't work, it's time to stop and analyze why and what might work better. Stay humane, but be creative. Is there a nonpunitive way to reach this child that you haven't tried before?

Remember, spanking is generally the last of a number of techniques for disciplining children. It's useful, but it's strong medicine, to be used sparingly. Whenever I think about the good news and the bad news about spanking, I think of Bert.

Bert was a middle-aged miner. He and his wife had begun having problems with their young son. Bert, though a strong, strapping man, had always been paralyzed when it came to using firmer forms of discipline like spanking. Sensing his father's unwillingness to limit him, and being strong-willed anyway, the son began testing his father more and more. Each time he did, the father capitulated.

The truth was that when he was a small boy, Bert was cruelly abused by his own father. He feared he could abuse his son as he was abused. As he told his wife, "I know I should probably spank the boy. But I just can't. I'm afraid that if I ever got started spanking him, I wouldn't be able to stop."

Bert had never read a professional book on child abuse. He did not know that according to statistics, people who have been abused as children tend to become abusers themselves. But every time he got mad at his son, he knew intuitively that he was at risk. He was doing all he knew to spare his son the tragedy he had experienced.

He was to be commended. Unfortunately, without firm discipline his son was floundering anyway. Bert's situation symbolizes for me that need for a balanced view toward spanking. Used appropriately and sparingly, spanking may help to direct a child whose impulses might not be channeled otherwise. If not used with the utmost of care, however, corporal punishment can turn into the vilest forms of abuse, leaving scars on both parents and children for generations to come.

15. *Be Creative*

If at first you don't succeed; try, try again. If you've tried and tried again, then try something else.

Parenting is *not* routine. Just about the time you think you have your discipline intact and your daily routine in order, your child will prove you don't.

It gets so bad in some families that the parents declare their kids are conspiring against them. Parents are sure they'll go to the back bedroom someday and catch big brother coaching junior.

"Look, junior," big brother will say. "Have you noticed how Mom and Dad are getting you to eat with all this positive reinforcement jazz? Telling you how proud they are when you eat your squash. It makes you want to just throw up!" he'll say as he sticks his finger into his mouth for a little extra emphasis.

"Now the next time they give you that squash, I want you to put some in your mouth and wait until they think you're really eating it. Then get that devilish look on your face—the one you used that time you threw your milk cup at grandma. Spit the squash all over the table. That'll get 'em to sit up and take notice!"

Most children don't really conspire against parents in this way. But children do fluctuate in how they respond to their parents.

There are several reasons. For one thing, children do test your limits. As children grow, they strive for greater and greater autonomy and independence. They want to see how far they can go. When you tell them they can't play in the street in front of your house, they may go out in the street at Grandma's house to see if you'll apply the rule there.

Children respond differently because they have their good and bad moments. The hungry child may be irritable and cranky. The same soothing that calmed him right after his meal yesterday doesn't work after four hours without food today.

We parents also have our good and bad days. That may cause our children to respond differently to us. If I'm under lots of stress and convey it to my children by being less patient and more punitive, they'll likely be the same way with me.

Children also respond differently because of their stage of development. Children are in a process of continual growth. They are like a fast growing shade tree. They put out new shoots. As they do, they continually change in form and shape. Many of these new developments represent positive change. They aid the tree's ability to give shade and stabilize the tree. But others grow in odd directions, or get in the way of the roof. These must be redirected or trimmed.

The successful parent of the developing child flexes to respond to the changing behavior of the child. I once knew a woman who loved the small toddlers she worked with at the nursery. They responded beautifully to her tremendous warmth and affection. They grew and learned with her like they would with no other.

But with teenagers she barely survived. She felt herself paralyzed by the sullen rebelliousness of that developmental stage. Lacking the assertiveness to respond firmly but fairly to the severe testing adolescents often put adults through, she was run over by them.

To parent an ever-changing child means that you learn and try new things. You must be willing to bend, to flex, to be creative.

The old saying goes, "If at first you don't succeed, try, try again." It's true. Perseverance is important. But in parenting we should add, "If you've tried and tried again, then for heaven's sake, try something else." Be creative. As someone once said, "If you've told your child a thousand times to do something and he hasn't done it, who's not listening?"

One night I was furious with our little five-year-old daughter. I don't even remember what the incident was about. I do remember it had been a very frustrating day and my daughter was acting out. The standard, stepwise disciplinary process—warning, time-out to the room, and a little extra yelling thrown in—didn't work. Finally, I spanked her.

But then I saw an angry look in her that was unlike anything I had ever seen. That look told me something was wrong. For some reason on this night, in this place, in these circumstances, the girl who usually understood and obeyed my "stepwise" discipline was not going to respond.

I did the right thing. I left her room. I stepped quickly into my bedroom and closed the door. I sat down on the bed. "What am I going to do?" I thought. I began catastrophizing. "This is terrible. What if she continues to act like that? What can I do?"

I tried to compose myself. "If you don't succeed, try something else!" I told myself. But what else was there to try? What else could I say?

There was nothing to say. Anything I said was going to escalate the problem.

Suddenly it hit me. What about writing?

That might deescalate the tension and still communicate. But how would I write any meaningful message to a five-year-old? Except for the most simple words, she could not read or write.

I got my paper out. After fumbling around, this is what I wrote:

I ♡ U.

U ARE 😠 AND 😢

ME 2.

LET'S TALK.

DAD

    I went to the desk, got a small envelope, and tucked the note inside. I went to her closed door, said a little prayer of hope, and slowly opened the door. She was laying on her bed and watched me out of the corner of her eye. I stepped quickly but quietly in, set the envelope on her bed, and left her room, closing the door.

    I went back to my bedroom and sat down on my bed to read. A few minutes went by. Then she came, quietly tiptoeing into the room. She crawled up on the bed and handed me the note.

    With tears in her eyes she said, "I love you, too, Daddy." She threw her arms around my neck. We just sat there quietly for a few moments.

    Then I said, "Do you want to talk now?"

    She nodded. We talked and worked out our differences.

    I dared to be creative at a difficult time. And the two of us, father and daughter, had grown.

16. *Finding Old Roots and Making New Ones*

*Let these stones be a memorial to what God has
done for you here, so that when your children ask,
"What do these old rocks mean?"
you'll be able to tell them.*

—Joshua 4:6-7, paraphrase

Yesterday, Joy and I found ourselves standing in an old grave-yard in Shreveport, Louisiana. We had come there with my mother to search for the graves of my great-grandfather and great-grandmother.

The search had become a family adventure. Several years before we had all come to this same cemetery looking for the graves. It had been almost sixty years since my mother had been there. While she found the cemetery with relative ease, she couldn't remember where the graves were.

I remember well our sitting together—my wife, Joy, her grand-mother, and me—in the old caretaker's house while the caretaker looked in vain through files of tattered and yellowed cards listing names and locations of the different burial plots. He recalled there had been a fire. When, he couldn't quite say. In the fire a lot of the old records had been destroyed. Apparently the location of the old graves was one of the things lost.

The old man pointed us in the direction of the oldest part of the cemetery. "Try over there," he said. "Maybe if the gravestones are still there and readable, you'll find them."

We spent much of the day looking. Little Joy stepped between gravestones with me until finally, tired from trying to keep up with her long-legged dad, she sat under the shade of an old tree to rest with her mother. We didn't find the graves that day.

Now, on this cool winter day, we had returned. This time we brought Mother's cousin with us. The cousin felt she could find the graves. Sure enough, within minutes she had led us to two aging markers underneath the spreading arms of a giant sycamore.

When we returned to the cousin's house, she went to a back room. She returned reverently carrying an old family Bible and a frayed picture album which she set on the table before Joy and my mother. Together we looked at the pictures. Afterward we shared a meal. Before we left, Mom's cousin again went to the back room and returned with several small family keepsakes. She gave one to each of us as tokens of our visit.

There was a time when extended families lived closer to each other. Brothers might work at the same business. Grandma and Grandpa might live no farther than the other side of the county.

At family gatherings, the elders sat around and told the old stories about family trials and triumphs, the funny moments and the one-of-a-kind happenings. The children, after hearing the stories countless times, would pick them up and eventually pass them on to their own children, keeping alive a kind of oral history of the family. To be sure, some stories bore only a romanticized resemblance to the actual facts. But the stories helped the family maintain a connectedness, not just between themselves but to past generations as well.

Now extended families are close if they live in the same state, let alone the same town. Immediate family members are involved in so many individual activities it's often hard to get Mom, Dad, and the kids together for a common meal, much less a reunion with relatives.

By the time youngsters are teenagers it may be nearly impossible to get extended families together with any regularity. That is why I believe you should do it when the children are young. It is especially good when they are in early grades in school.

Of course, finding out about their roots is more interesting to some children than others. I don't believe in forcing children to spend hours being bored. But with a little ingenuity, you can make things more interesting.

Can you think of anything about the family roots that you believe would interest them? Young girls are often fascinated by weddings. They might enjoy looking at pictures of an old marriage ceremony. Some boys are intrigued by stories of courage and adventure. They might enjoy visiting with and looking through the memorabilia of an older male relative. Many children like to look at pictures of their grandparents when they were children to see what it was like to be a child in the "good old days."

Older and younger generations need each other. They provide each other with a special kind of nurture that can't be found elsewhere. As the younger generation matures, they begin to recognize and understand not just the genealogical factors that link them to the past but the psychological ones as well. People are often interested in their medical inheritance—family predispositions toward heart disease and the like. Hopefully as families reestablish themselves across generations, they'll become interested in their psychological inheritance as well.

Now uncovering old memories is important—but so is making new ones. The things you and your children do today are the potential memories of tomorrow. Each generation puts down new roots.

What makes an event memorable in a young child's mind?

Contrary to what adults think, it has little to do with the "greatness" of the event. Children often remember things that seem insignificant to us. Children remember most the times—whether great or small—spent in fellowship with the important people in their lives. They remember events which tell them they have special worth to these people.

When I was about five, I used to wait every day at the end of the driveway for my dad to come home from work. Each day I'd see him turn into the gravel road that led to our drive. As I watched him get closer and closer, I'd get more and more excited to see him and tell him about my day.

Those were special times, but one day in particular stands out. When Dad got home that day, he got out of the car and handed me a brand-new shiny Spalding softball. I was ecstatic. I felt like jumping the hedge and yelling out loud.

I was excited, but to be honest, I didn't care much for softball then. I had been to one ball game in my life and found the organist and the peanut vendor more interesting than anything happening on the field. What made that softball special was that my dad had taken time out from his work, which I figured was pretty important, and had gone to the store to get that ball for *me*!

He had remembered me even when we were not physically together. That meant I was important to him. Somehow my heart knew this gift had nothing to do with ball games. It had everything to do with love. That was what excited me.

Families make memories together when they do things together. On a Friday evening we can turn off "Wall Street Week" and get everybody in the kitchen to make cookies together. We'll get flour on the floor and the cookies may not be great, but we'll be together, laughing and cutting up.

Cameras can help children lock in special memories and start their becoming "memory collectors." Obviously, this isn't practical for toddlers, but most children by the time they reach age six can be taught to handle a simple camera.

After they've gained experience, give them a roll of film. Tell them to take pictures of anything that interests them. It's fascinating to see the way they frame their shots—the people and poses they include. When you see the first picture of yourself, you'll realize how much taller and bigger you look from a child's perspective. Notice facial expressions the child catches on film.

Sometimes children are better at capturing people's feelings on film than adults are. Adults tend to take posed, grin-and-bear-it shots. Children see the value in candid pictures of Dad lying down on the couch watching TV or Mom working in the garden. Such pictures provide children with an album full of memories taken from their unique perspective.

Traditions, things done more than once, can also lock in memories in the young child's mind. Again, these events don't have to be earth-shaking. An annual trip to Disneyland could be alright, but a monthly trip to a special café for sodas might be better.

Somewhere on the east side of Houston, this side of the shipping docks and the other side of the coffee plant, there used to be a café like that. It was one of those places with a few formica tables, a lunch counter, and a small sign out front to identify the place. I think it was one of those signs paid for by the soft drink company, because most of the sign was taken up by the soda water logo. Only a small space was left along the bottom for the name of the establishment.

It wasn't much of a place, but it meant something to me when I was a young boy. Often on Saturdays my dad would have to take care of some business at the warehouse where he worked. And often he would let me go with him. He'd do his work and I'd either play or do minor chores for him.

After we finished at the warehouse, we'd sometimes go over to that little café to get something to drink. Dad would usually have coffee; I took to ordering a lemon-lime soda.

Occasionally, someone Dad knew would be in the café. They'd come over. "How you doin', G. A.?" they'd say. "This your boy? Fine lookin' boy you got there, G. A." Mostly though, it was just Dad and me passing the time, sipping our drinks, and talking about this and that.

Somehow I always thought the lemon-lime soda was better in that old café. Back then, I believed it was because of the clear glasses it was served in and some special way the bubbles sparkled in the glass. But that logic failed me when I'd get back home. We had lemon-lime soda in clear glasses at home and it sparkled there, too. But somehow it just wasn't the same.

Now I understand.

17. Enter the Inner World

If one feels the needs of something grand ... one need not go far to find it. I think I see something deeper, more infinite, more eternal than the ocean in the expression of the eyes of a little baby when it wakes in the morning and coos or laughs because it sees the sun shining on its cradle.

—Vincent Van Gogh

Six-year-old Joy was watching her nine-month-old niece Lauren crawl on the living room floor. At intervals, Lauren would stare at a trinket across the floor from where she lay. A little smile would cross her lips. Then, with a start, she would set her mouth and scoot further across the floor toward the object.

"Daddy, wouldn't it be neat if we could tell what Lauren's thinking?" Joy asked. Indeed it would. It would be great if we could enter the private world of the child and understand what ticks inside those tiny heads.

To some extent, child researchers have done this. With various experiments, they can surmise something of what it's like to see the world through a child's eyes. We know for example, that even small babies prefer to look at a drawing of a friendly human face rather than at other figures (Fantz, 1961).

We know that if you put a wide glass of water and a thin glass of water in front of a five-year-old and ask him to pick the one with the most water, he'll invariably pick the tallest one. He doesn't yet understand that he must take the width of the glass into consideration when trying to determine the volume of water inside. He'll be about seven before he understands that (Rubin and Fisher, 1982, pp. 29-31).

Most of us aren't child researchers. We aren't going to set up laboratories and analyze our children through one-way mirrors. Yet we can come to understand more about what's going on inside our children's minds. They'll allow us into their inner worlds if we take the time to enter with love and respect.

A good way to gain entry is to sit back and observe. It's amazing how many new discoveries we can watch our children make when we turn off the TV, put down the paper, hang up the phone, and just watch them do what kids do. Like a preschool Einstein, your child is making all kinds of new discoveries every day. It's intriguing, exciting, and sometimes just plain fun to watch the way they do it.

Watch your children playing by themselves. Listen to the things they tell imaginary friends when playing their solitary games. Watch them interact with other children and adults. Try not to be obtrusive. Just fade into the surroundings.

My girls have some of those toy microphones—replicas of the kind the big stars use. Occasionally one of them will take her microphone in the bathroom, close the door, and give an impromptu concert before the mirror. I've never been in the bathroom for one of these performances, but the lyrics, mostly made up as she goes along, can often be heard through the door. These lyrics give fascinating clues about what the girls are thinking.

On a certain day, one girl made up a new song. Before the day was over both girls were marching around the house singing it as they stepped in time. It went something like this.

If you're feeling kinda blue
And you don't know what to do
Call on God
Call on God!

Observation is one way to gain entry into the inner world. Conversation and direct interaction is another. The setting is important if you want your child really to open up. Relaxed, laid-back moments are especially conducive. Driving alone in the car together, a quiet time before bed—these are fine times to talk.

Not just any interaction will do. As you talk together, see yourself not as a teacher, leader, or instructor. There's a place for all those roles in parenting, but not when you are entering the inner world. Put yourself in your child's shoes. As you listen, try to see the world as she sees it and convey to her that you do.

As she opens up, keep empathizing. Don't suddenly start preaching to her because she brought up something you decided deserved a good lecture. If you pounce on her when she finally gets to the point of opening up, you'll make her feel she can't trust you with her innermost thoughts. Give her a chance. There's a time to talk instruction. But right now, just listen.

As you talk, put into words those things that will let her know you are seeing through her eyes. If she's talking about something frightening, say, "That must have felt scary!" If she's telling about the bully at school, recall a bully in your own life. Don't be too quick to tell her what to do about the bully. Start just by letting her know you understand what a situation like that is like.

These times with your child will do wonders for the relationship. You'll come to know your child better. And she'll feel she knows you better. You'll be cementing the relationship.

We were having bedtime prayers one night, my two daughters and me. We sat close together on the bed. My oldest began, then my four-year-old. Always before, the little one had tucked her head shyly in her pillow, praying in inaudible whispers, perhaps unsure whether what she had to say was worth saying to us— much less to God. This night, however, she stood up to pray and spoke with conviction. She had something important to say to God.

"God," she began, "thank you for Mommy and Joy and Daddy. And God," she paused. "If Daddy should kick all his covers off in the middle of the night, help him pull them back up so he can be comfortable. Amen."

What made that prayer special to me wasn't just its cuteness. It's what it said about what was important to my daughter as a four-year-old. It put me in touch with a forgotten memory. When I was a young boy, I too felt the discomfort of waking up in the middle of a cold night, with all my blankets off the end of the bed and my cold knees tightly clutched against my chest. I remember feeling warm and thankful when Momma would come in like a guardian angel in the dark night and draw the soft covers back under my chin. Then I knew why Alicia prayed that prayer. And I was thankful—thankful that I had once again been allowed a brief vision into her inner world.

18. *The Early Evening Battlefield*

Better times are coming . . .

—an unknown soldier

It's 5:30 p.m. You, the dedicated father, are driving home from a disastrous day at work. You are destined for the tranquility of your happy home. What a relief to be home, you think, as you turn into the driveway. You're halfway up the sidewalk when loud shouting penetrates the walls of the house.

"Give it back, you dodo brain!" Junior is yelling to his little brother. You walk in just in time to see Junior rip the ball out of little brother's hands. Little brother collapses on the floor, draws a deep breath, and lets out a shriek that would send General Patton running for cover.

Your harried wife races by yelling something about how she's ready to scream. Then as she's leading Junior by the ear to his room, she says if you want dinner tonight you better do something about *your* kids.

Suddenly you have an overwhelming desire to go back to the office. The office was easier.

Or maybe both of you work. Add to the chaos stressors from two offices, school, and daycare, and the mix turns even more explosive.

In many households, the hours between 5:00-7:00 p.m. are a battlefield. Children are tired. One parent has been in the house all day with pint-sized helpers or has been on the job. The other parent has fought the job and the freeway. Everyone is hungry. It's a wonder we don't declare the whole country a police state during the hours of five and seven.

Dealing with the family battlefield, especially when some "bombs" are aimed directly at you, requires conscious commitment. Family stress can sometimes, though not always, be anticipated. If experience tells you that the odds of the whole family being stressed at 5:30 in the evening is high, you can start to prepare for it. If you are driving home from work, you can begin to decompress in the car. You can loosen your tie or hair, turn on easy-listening radio, and purposefully avoid mimicking the intense style of your fellow drivers.

You can begin to think realistically about what you will face when you get home. Thinking realistically doesn't mean being cynical. It doesn't mean assuming the kids will be hanging from the chandeliers or setting fire to the car. Neither does it mean being Pollyannish, deluding yourself into believing you'll come home to find spouse and children sitting quietly by the fireplace sipping hot chocolate, singing the gentle strains of "There's No Place Like Home."

Sometimes when coming home I remind myself that the challenges at home will be different from the ones at work. I know from studies in stress management that even stress can be rejuvenating so long as it's a different kind of stress. I also think of the ways in which being at home will be preferable to being at work. Let's face it. Most jobs aren't easy either. It's just that we usually expect a job to be tough, while we expect home to be a place of quiet serenity. Sometimes when driving home I think of ways dealing with home problems will actually be a nice change of pace from problems I've been dealing with at the office all day.

Sometimes I remind myself that after the battlefield time is over, things will get calmer. I think about some creative game or activity my children and I could enjoy together before bed, and that helps me get through the battlefield hour.

I also remind myself that home is less stressful if I treat it as a place to get involved in rather than a place to crash. Many people have the mistaken impression that in the best "Home, Sweet, Home" you can turn your mind off at the front door. Nothing could be further from the truth. Home is a place of rest, but it is also a place of participation. Homelife never improves when the leaders in the family treat it with benign neglect.

But what if you happen to be a harried houseparent who has been with children much of the day? You can, if the children are old enough, require that they play alone during late afternoon hours. This avoids sibling conflicts and frees you to sit down, take a deep breath, and renew your spirits. Take time for a snack—but not junk food. Eat something nutritious—an orange, an apple— something that rejuvenates. Make sure the children have something to hold them until dinner too.

Have the children rest when their fatigue has reached the point of explosive irritability. Often it is not necessary to require children to lay down. Just have them choose several games to play or books to read and put them in a quiet place. The quiet time will help them rejuvenate and make it through the rest of the day.

When you and your spouse first meet, take each others' "emotional temperature." Find out how the other is feeling. Don't ask for an exhaustive replay of the whole day. Just exchange reports on how you are each doing emotionally and how that affects what you both will do with the evening ahead.

Who's going to take responsibility for taking care of the children during the battlefield hours? Who's going to bite the bullet and take responsibility for things anyway? Sometimes you have to find a way to get by even when neither of you feels like it. But at least if you talk, you'll be more unified in your effort.

Of course early evening isn't the only time when families are on the brink of disintegrating. Anytime all members of the family are under intense physical or emotional stress, coping is hard. Being a supportive, helpful family is always easier when things are calm. When life piles up on you, it's hard to be responsive to others.

Some family stress can't be anticipated. The child who comes down with the flu right when you are about to make a big trip. The child who always takes naps and now won't go to sleep despite being cranky as an old troll.

But many family stressors can be anticipated using past experience as a guide. If you know the odds are ten to one that taking Junior on a seven-hour car trip will make him a raging bull next day, you can protect your best china and batten down the hatches.

Whatever you do, don't ignore potential stress times. Remember, these are not times to become overly optimistic. Cautious realism is the key. Suppose your daughter wants to invite a friend over to play this afternoon. You know that this twosome usually requires close parental supervision. This is the last day you can do your taxes. You do not need frequent interruptions.

At times like this, some parents, knowing the potential problems, will succumb to the child's request anyway. They'll tell themselves that things will go better this time. Or they'll be able to cope with any distractions. Don't do it. Family stress times are no time to stick your head in the sand.

Above all, keep the faith. You may be in the middle of the family battlefield right now. But be of good cheer. Better times are coming. Hang in there.

19. *Limit Them*

*Children need parents who can tell them
how far is far enough.*

Children want limits. No child will tell you that out loud. But they do.

In sixth grade I was a member of the school safety patrol. The school was middle-class, filled with mostly average kids. Each year our sponsor, Mr. Carley, took all the patrol boys on an overnight camp-out to the lake. It was our reward for a year of good work.

Rumor had it that at this camp-out, you could stay up all night, roam the park, and do most anything you wanted. For weeks the boys bragged about how great it would be to hang out all night, something no self-respecting mother allowed her son to do in our neighborhood.

When the day of the camp-out came, emotions were running high. This was the night all the boys were waiting for.

We drove to the lake, ate our supper, and had a meeting by the campfire. About ten that night, Mr. Carley crawled into the back-seat of his car. He threw a blanket over himself and went to sleep. He didn't say anything. He didn't command us to go to sleep or scare us about how we'd get acne if we didn't go to sleep. He just got in his car and went to sleep.

In the beginning we were ecstatic. We had the camp to ourselves. We ran wild. At first we played organized games, but as the night wore on, the games degenerated. Some boys threw rocks at each other. Others had knife-throwing contests. Boys who tried to go to sleep were attacked.

As the night went on, I grew tired and irritable. I felt sick. I wished I was at home in my bed. Most of all, I wished with all my heart that Mr. Carley would get up and make us go to bed. I felt out of control. It did not feel good. At the time, I could never have put these feelings into words. But that is what I felt.

People who grew up with alcoholic parents tell me they constantly experienced chaos like that. That's because alcoholic parents are so clouded by their drinking they provide no limits or inconsistent limits. Or they maintain control through abuse.

Childhood is a time of tension between two poles. On the one hand, the child wants to grow, to create, to try new things, to walk as far as he can, to see how things work. He experiments with crayons on paper, and he might want to see how they would look on a freshly painted wall. He rides tricycles on the sidewalk and may also want to know what it would feel like to ride one on the street.

On the other hand, children want stability. They want to know that someone will keep them from getting into danger.

In many ways, this tension exists throughout life. But in childhood it takes on special relevance, because children really don't know how far is safe for them. They may have vague ideas. Like the toddler just learning to walk, they may relish the idea of walking to the end of the sidewalk. But they may just as suddenly feel and obey an inner urge to run back to the security of the front porch where mother waits with open arms.

Children need parents to help define how far is enough. Just when does staying up late become late enough? That's too gray an issue for a young child to decide. Only a parent, with an understanding of what time really means and what is finally good for a child's health, can decide such issues. Parents relinquish responsibility nature dictates when they avoid limiting their children.

Limiting can be overdone. Children who are overly controlled do not have freedom to test their independence in slow, deliberate steps. Parents who fear for their well-being and overprotect them prevent their finding their own way in the world. Or parents with a strong need for power themselves cannot allow their children the freedom to grow up.

Overcontrolled children often end up depressed or rebellious. The depressed child has lost hope that he can get out from under the watchful eyes of his parents. He surrenders to their domination. The aggressive child attacks parents who have controlled him, seeking in desperation to break their stranglehold.

The child whose parents give him a balance of limits and independence learns to be secure in the knowledge that his parents will intervene when he gets too far out on a limb. These children learn that pushing forward can be harmful when it hurts you or other people. They learn that venturing ahead can be wonderful when it leads to discovery, invention, and fulfillment. Over time, they learn how to use their own judgment to decide when to push forward into unchartered territory and when not.

20. *Train Up a Child . . .*

Let the children come to me . . . for the Kingdom of God belongs to such as these.

—Jesus Christ (Mark 10:14)

One of the saddest things about living in our times is the degree to which we have lost our way in pursuit of living faith and morals that work. In our understandable fervor to insure that the educational system not discriminate against any one group, we run the risk of raising children with no spiritual concepts at all. Misguided efforts to make teaching amoral may lead to an increased incidence of children who are immoral.

Most people in this country don't actively denigrate spiritual and moral development. They just neglect them. As a result, modern children lack basic concepts that many adults learned so early they take them for granted.

Recently I struggled to share with a group of fourth-graders why one would want to do a service project for someone else without getting paid. They could understand that you might do it for your parents because your parents would "make" you. But the idea that you might actually help someone for charity—why would anyone want to do that?

Cultivating children's moral and spiritual development begins at home. Our church can help us and we should seek help there. But individual Christian parents must be involved too.

Some parents feel uncomfortable here. They feel insecure about their own spirituality and thus unsure about how to help their children.

That's alright. Becoming parents has encouraged many adults to examine their own spiritual condition with resulting benefit to both parent and child.

It's never too early to start. I remember the week after three-year-old Alicia learned to sing "Jesus Loves Me" (actually it was more of a singsong chant). All the way to church next Sunday she chanted the song in different styles and with different emphases.

First it was soft, then it was loud, then strong and commanding, then soft and sweet. First, it was "*Jesus* loves me," then it was "Jesus *loves* me," then it was "Jesus loves *ME!*" Suddenly her inflection, the intensity of her voice, and the smile on her face told me she had caught the concept. The person that we call God loved *her!* What a massive insight for such a tiny girl.

In helping children with their faith, I've tried to remember that they go through stages in their ability to understand religious concepts. Small children think concretely about God. They don't understand abstract concepts like the Trinity. They don't fathom lots of analogies.

You can't tell a little child to "let his [or her] light shine" (Matt. 5:16) or to be "the salt of the earth" (Matt. 5:13) and expect him to know what you mean. You could try. You could bring in a flashlight or a shaker of salt to illustrate your point. You might get him to memorize, then "parrot" some of these concepts back to you. But if you expect the child to really get the idea that he is to be a good example to others, you're "barking up the wrong tree," so to speak.

What small children do understand are the basics. They can learn that

God loves them and cares for them (1 Peter 5:7)
God is always with them (Matt. 28:20)
God made them (Gen. 1:27)
They should please and obey God in what they do (Ps. 18:1)
God made the world (Gen. 1:1)
God provides for our needs (sun, rain, food, etc.)
God wants us to love and help one another (1 John 4:7)

When I answer a small child's questions about God, I try to orient my answers toward basic concepts they're likely to understand (Ballard & Fleck, 1975).

Above all, I want my children to know God loves them and that they are special to him. One of my favorite Bible stories for young children is Mark 10:13-16. In the story, some parents brought their children to see Jesus. The disciples try to shoo the children away. Jesus doesn't have time to fool around with runny-nosed kids, they reason. He's talking theology and the real issues of life.

In a radical move for a time when children were thought of as little more than possessions, Jesus not only refuses to send the children away. He invites them to be with him. He takes them in his arms and blesses them. Children are important to God.

Teaching children about God goes beyond memorizing platitudes. It means applying the great truths spontaneously to everyday experience.

I recall an African American minister who had a tremendous practical command of the Bible yet had not learned to read until nearly an adult. When asked how he did it, he said that when he was a child, he worked with his father on a farm. Throughout the day his father would relate things that they did, and problems they faced, to stories in the Bible. So powerful were these living applications of the biblical message that the words of Scripture became fixed in the young man's mind even though he had never read the book himself.

As children get older, they can also learn to act out their faith in everyday action. I want my children to do more than believe concepts. Contrary to popular opinion, research shows that strongly held beliefs do not necessarily translate into behaviors which demonstrate that belief. In other words, people who profess strongly to being Christians and have a lot of Christian knowledge don't necessarily act like Christians in their daily life.

Beliefs have to be translated into action. People who learn to act on their beliefs have those beliefs solidified. Belief and action become wedded. In some churches, people who come to believe in Jesus as the Christ and seek membership in the church are asked to make a public profession of their faith. This initial action helps the person solidify their newly stated belief. Children who learn about sharing in their Sunday school class and then get involved in a sharing project are more likely to share again.

Prayer is another way small children develop spiritual life. There is a place for rote prayers. But to become truly meaningful to a child prayer will eventually come close to what it really is—talking to God. Prayer at its richest is a conversation. Through prayer, I express my gratitude, my feelings, my needs and concerns, my hope and trust. Children need to know that while God expects certain behavior from them, they are free to express any feeling to him. They need to know that whether they need to share joy or sorrow, pleasure or anger, they can be totally honest with God.

Christian author Keith Miller (1967) recalls one night when he was having bedtime prayers with his five-year-old. Keith had been crabby at the dinner table that night. Knowing he was wrong, Keith confessed in prayer that he was sorry and wanted God to help him do better. When it was his five-year-old's turn to pray, there was a long silence. Then with eyes clenched shut she said, "Dear God, forgive me for teeteeing out in the backyard last summer."

When we pray like this, child, parent and God grow closer together. Here again though prayer begins where the child is. The small child's understanding of prayer isn't fully developed. If the child is more comfortable with rote prayers at times, we can be flexible enough to accommodate.

Finally, children learn moral and spiritual concepts from their parents' example. In fact, your example is the most significant way you teach these concepts. In an important study on what makes children share, two researchers found that there is *nothing more powerful than the example of an adult who herself demonstrates sharing* (Rosenhan & White, 1967).

If you live out your faith in practice, it is more likely your children will also. Of course some children react negatively to their parents' faith model. But that is most likely to happen where the parents' faith is rigid, cruel, or has little meaning to the child. Or where there is a big chasm between what the parents say they believe and what they actually live out.

If a parent's faith is alive and well, its example carries a powerful message. If your faith gives your life real meaning and purpose it's likely to offer your children the same.

21. That Kid's Face Looks Familiar

Sometimes our children have personality traits . . .
we just don't like.

Some of us enter parenthood with heads full of happy memories of the people in our past. Others have memories which are anything but happy.

Coach Larson was my seventh-grade gym coach. I had the misfortune of having Larson at a time when a lisp made it difficult for me to pronounce the letter "S."

Coach loved to come through the boy's locker room and shout at me in front of all the other boys. "Hey boy, what's your name again?" he'd ask with a sadistic little grin on his face.

"Sthanders, sthir," I'd answer as quietly as possible.

"What did you say?" he would call out.

"Sthanders," I'd reply, louder, but still trying hard to hide my face behind my locker door.

"Oh yeah, Sthanders. That's right," he'd say. Then he'd walk away chuckling, leaving me to face the teasing of my classmates.

I endured Coach Larson for a year. Then I was through with his class and would never have to suffer through his little game again. When Coach Larson died a few years later I experienced for the first time those strange ambivalent feelings we all have when someone who has hurt us dies.

Some people struggle for years with a hurtful person much closer to them than a Coach Larson. It may be a mother who can't stay away from a bottle. A father who hurts them or sexually abuses them. A mother who seems to turn the other way when they try to tell her their problems. Or a brother who teases them unmercifully.

Helen had a mother that never could seem to get very interested in her. Other things energized her mother, but not Helen. She was concerned about civic and political affairs. But she never got to Helen's class play, the Christmas pageant, or the children's choir. She seemed to have time for new hairstyles and make-overs but no time for playing beauty shop with her daughter. When she did take time to be with her, her eyes always seemed far away.

Helen's mother died several years ago and Helen experienced her ambivalence. She could hardly put a name to the feelings. She knew she loved her mother very much. But she knew part of her also hated her mother.

She understood intellectually that her mother did things the only way she knew. But when a person hurts you it causes pain, even when the other person has a good excuse. Helen's mother hurt her a lot. When she died, a part of Helen grieved and suffered in anguish. Another part felt relieved that, at last, her mother could no longer hurt her. Still another part felt guilty because she *was* relieved.

Now though, Helen has a daughter named Melissa. Melissa seems so much like Helen's mother that yesterday Helen called her by her mother's name. How could this have happened? Helen swore she was going to be nothing like her mother. She thought she had succeeded—only to find that her own daughter is the spitting image of Momma. What kind of ugly trick has God played?

Melissa starts complaining about "having to have" the perfect clothes and the perfect hairstyle. Helen hears echoes of the times her mother's hair appointments seemed the most important priorities on the planet. When Helen looks at her daughter's face, it is as if her mother's face is superimposed on the face of this child.

Now Helen is angry not at her mother but at the daughter who dares to act so much like her. When Helen isn't angry, she's worried. She worries that nothing she does will spare her daughter from becoming a carbon copy of her grandmother.

All of us see people who remind us of others. It's particularly devastating when one of your children reminds you of a painful relationship from your past.

The Coach Larsons that I meet in my life today set off reactions inside me that occur long before such people do anything to hurt me. I become defensive even when there's no cause for alarm. A part of me thinks of ways I can protect myself from their hurt and a part of me wants to make a "first strike" against them.

These situations are difficult for a parent. They are no less difficult for a child.

One boy, Harvey, felt bewildered by his mother's reaction to him. She found fault with most everything he did. If there was any doubt, she blamed him anyway. She seemed to be daring Harvey to rebel and, in rebelling, to reject her.

What Harvey didn't know was that he favored his mother's father. Throughout her childhood, Harvey's mother had felt rejected by her dad. Unconsciously, she felt that since Harvey was so much like his granddad, he would probably reject her too. So she treated Harvey like the enemy she expected him to become.

Unfortunately, Harvey understood none of this. So, when he had finally had enough of his mother's unremitting criticism, reject her he did. Harvey's mother was unable to see her son as a unique individual. She thus condemned herself and Harvey to a self-fulfilling prophecy.

Sometimes our children don't remind us of anyone particular in our pasts. Yet they may have personality traits we just don't like. From the day they are born, all children seem to come with certain character traits, some more pleasant to deal with than others. For example, some children are more docile and easygoing while others enter the world with loud cries and strong wills.

Kevin was a child whose personality was not heaven sent. While the rest of his brothers and sisters were playing with dolls and baseballs, Kevin was searching for the closest animal he could torture. Frogs and insects were his victims of choice. His poor mother had never seen anything like it. She wondered if her son was predestined to be an armed guard in a concentration camp.

Children like Kevin are hard to deal with. Faced with them, we parents have an understandable tendency to throw up our hands. "This is just the way my boy is," we say. "He has always been sort of mean" (or stubborn or rude or aloof).

Having done this, we settle down to cope with his personality, and we pray to God that our boy's shortcomings of character won't get him into too much trouble someday. Whenever he pulls the legs off another innocent frog, we discipline him. And while we're at it we say, "Kevin, why are you so mean! Are you *always* going to be this way?" Each time we say that, we are telling him we have lost hope that he will ever change.

Maybe you have a Kevin or a Harvey or a Melissa at your house. If so, you need extra help. Help is available. It requires that you stop right now and see a side of yourself and your child that your frustration has blinded you to.

Sit quietly for a moment. Close your eyes. As you do, visualize your problem child standing in a row of children. At the front of the line, a sign says, "Children with handicaps. Will you help them overcome their handicap?"

You look down the row. Each child has a sign hung around his or her neck. The sign on one child reads, "blind." The one on the next child reads "wheelchair bound." Other signs say "slow reader" or "shy."

Now you come to your child. Look closely at the sign. On it is written the name of the personality trait you dislike. It could be stubbornness, aggressiveness, rudeness. Can you see your child in this way? What kind of feelings does this arouse in you? Does it change the way you think about your child's "problem"?

Chances are you've just thought about your child's personality deficit as something that needs your help rather than your helplessness. That personality problem is real—but is not written in stone. In fact, as the parent of a young child, you have more to say about it than anyone else ever will.

So what can you do about it? First, admit to yourself that the child's personality trait is a real turnoff for you. It has been and at times will continue to be.

Now focus all your attention on the personality trait opposite to the one bothering you. If your child is stubborn, think about cooperative behaviors. If your child is mean, think of caring behaviors.

Make a point to watch your child more than usual. Don't be obtrusive. Just keep watch. Now every time you see behavior you like, the polar opposite of one you dislike, praise him. If you catch him sharing his toys with another boy, come up and tell him so. Don't embarrass him. And above all don't tell him you're glad he's *finally* learning to share. Just say, "I like it when you share your toys like that." Give him a smile and a pat on the back.

When your child is exhibiting the personality trait you don't like, tell him firmly the behaviors you expect from him. Don't remind him of the things you dislike.

Instead of

"Why do you always have to be grabbing your little brother's toys? You are so terrible! Now go in your room and stay there."

Say,

"I want you to leave the room for grabbing your brother's toys. Then, as soon as you are ready, I want you to come back out and show me how you play with him cooperatively."

Consider one other thing. Some personality traits are clearly problems. A tendency to hurt others is not good; the child needs to be encouraged toward more positive traits. However, some traits aren't necessarily bad in themselves. Melissa was concerned about her appearance, but did that mean she would neglect others as her grandmother had? Not necessarily. Sometimes in our worry that a child will be "just like" an ancestor we condemn her for things that are only superficially similar.

Dealing with a "familiar face" presents a challenge. If you are the parent of such a child, perhaps this prayer will have meaning for you.

Lord:
You have entrusted me with a child, who through no fault of his own, awakens painful memories and elicits anticipatory fears inside of me. I confess, there are things about him I do not like.

Help me accept my child for the unique person that he is. At the same time, remind me daily that accepting my child, does not mean accepting behaviors that will doom him to failure.

As I grow, give me strength to facilitate his growth. Give me wisdom to shape his young character so that he may grow naturally toward the light rather than the darkness. And, I pray that as I grow in relationship with him, I will find healing for the painful memories of my own past.

Amen

22. The Language of Feelings

In a young child, a feeling is an energy force in its rawest form.

It was late in the afternoon. Alicia's sister woke her prematurely from her nap.

Nothing would suit her. She wanted to play, but she couldn't find the right toy. She didn't want to go outside, but she really didn't want to stay in. She was exasperated . . . and angry. Four-year-olds have trouble with their anger.

When I came on the scene, she was standing in front of an open closet whining and moaning. She couldn't find a box into which to put a picture she had drawn to give her sister as a present.

I pulled a box from the closet. "This box will work if you roll the picture up like this," I said, naively thinking this would placate her.

"No!" she shrieked. "Get it out of there. It's gonna bend it all up!"

"Well, what about this box?" I said, pointing to a slightly bigger one. "You'd only have to curl it this much to get it in here."

"No, that dummy thing won't work either! Nothing works! Nothing ever works!" with that she collapsed on the floor of the hall with her head buried in the carpet.

Within each child there is a world of feelings and emotions. This feeling world includes all the emotions known to human-kind: joy, peace, anxiety, shame, rage, hatred, envy, sympathy, tenderness, happiness, and hopelessness, to name only a few.

The language of feelings is spoken in a variety of ways. It may be verbal. But in the young child it is as likely to be expressed through facial expression, body language, or physical action. The child who just dove into the pool successfully for the first time, and bounces to the surface with a huge grin on her face, is telling you something about her feelings.

A little boy with a pouty face crouched in the corner of the backseat of the car is telling you more than words ever could. And a child gritting her teeth and pushing another child off a chair is making a strong statement even if no words are spoken.

In a young child, a feeling is an energy force in its rawest form. It is powerful and sometimes totally unrestrained. It can be wonderful. What does it feel like when a three-year-old wakes up on Christmas morning to find his presents under the tree? Many adults only wish they could again attain the levels of rapture innocent children experience.

Sometimes the intensity of their feelings goes to their heads. They feel a sense of power and omnipotence that would make a demagogue blush. People who dare get in their way are shouted down and shoved aside. "Please and thank you" go by the wayside. Others are expected to follow their orders without question. Even elders are fair game.

But the raw power of their feelings can frighten and confuse children, too. Every day the young child is experiencing inner urges, many of which she has no name for. She hasn't learned that the intense negative feeling she has for her new baby brother is called jealousy. She may be overwhelmed by conflicting inner impulses that tell her to mother the new baby at one moment and throw him in the trash can the next. Conflicting feelings of haughtiness and affection may cause her to hit you over the head with a book this morning and cuddle with you this afternoon.

Sometimes a child like this seems implicitly to welcome having an adult step in, offer discipline, and restore control over the child's chaotic emotions. Like a patient brought back from the throes of delirium, she is thankful someone helped her take charge of her faculties again.

A child can also become overwhelmed by pleasant emotions. He may become so excited, so happy, that he has trouble maintaining any sense of judgment. Whenever my daughter got together with another boy her age, they used to get so excited they'd go wild. Seeing each other was like setting off happy hour. They'd start giggling like two people exposed to laughing gas. They'd chase each other here and there without caring whether they were in the middle of a busy parking lot or safely behind the fence at home.

Feelings are an important part of a child's life. Properly channeled, they are a dynamic source of energy that empowers children to learn and grow.

How can you help your child make the most of his feelings? First, observe your child. Learn his unspoken feeling language. How does he act when he gets envious, or mad, or embarrassed?

Sometimes it's obvious, as when the proud child struts her new Halloween costume around the living room for all to see. Sometimes it's not so easy. One mother was perplexed when her five-year-old reacted to the death of his cat with a day full of black humor. "Well, that cat is mincemeat now," he chuckled cynically to the chagrin of both Mom and Dad.

But the next day, when they had the cat's "funeral," the same boy burst into tears and clung to his mother's neck. His mother suddenly realized that the black humor did not reflect lack of sympathy. It was an attempt to cover up the tremendous amount of inner grief the boy really felt.

Help your child begin to identify his feelings. If he's sad tell

him, "You seem sad to me." Instead of calling other people bad
names, encourage him to say, "I'm mad at you!" When he wants to
hit you, tell him to say, "I feel like hitting you!" He won't always
say it, but he'll begin to get the idea.

A great way to teach young children to identify and express
their emotions is the "feeling wheel" developed by developmental
psychologists Joseph and Laurie Braga (1976). Take a paper plate,
or cut out a piece of cardboard in the shape of a circle. Around the
circle draw simple faces displaying different emotions as shown
below.

This copy of a drawing from *Children and Adults*, by Joseph and Laurie Braga,
is used by permission.

Now cut out a cardboard pointer. Use a brad to hold it in the
center of the circle. Attach the feeling wheel to the door of your
child's room. As you do, explain to the child in a pleasant way that
whenever she feels sad and wants to tell you, she can turn the
pointer to the sad face.

Point to each face. Describe each one. Tell her that when she is feeling mean or angry she can turn the pointer to those feelings. This will help her tell you without her using rough words or hitting someone. It is best, of course, to explain all this to the child while she's in a good mood.

The feeling wheel can be helpful to children as young as four. Even though they can't read the words, most can figure out the expressions on the drawings well enough to use them.

Identifying emotions and using a feeling wheel can help children demystify their feelings, make them less scary. This helps the child build confidence that he can gain control over his feelings. It is important in helping the child channel his emotions toward constructive purposes.

Empathize with your child's feelings. See the world through her eyes. Imagine what kind of feelings you would have if you were looking at the world as she is.

That afternoon when Alicia was so exasperated, I looked down at her curled up with her thumb in her mouth. I thought about myself. Earlier that day, I got angry when I accidentally printed a letter wrong on my last piece of personal stationery. I wadded the letter up into a tight little ball and threw it so hard at the wastebasket it flew past the trash, out the door, and into the next room. At the time, my day felt ruined by one lousy letter. As I looked at Alicia, I saw a little girl's version of the same emotion.

With that, I lay down on the floor next to her. I was tentative. I didn't try to touch because sometimes when she's angry touches are too much and she hits back or pushes away. I wanted to avoid getting into a disciplinary episode about the wrongness of hitting parents. I hoped to stick just to the issue at hand.

So I just lay there on the floor of the hallway of my house, a little behind her, not even looking at her. Then I quietly said, "You seem so upset, Alicia. You seem so angry."

I waited a few seconds. She lay still.

"Sometimes I get really angry too, when nothing seems to work the way I want it to."

She turned her head ever so slightly toward me.

"I wanted a box that would fit. I don't *want* to fold up my picture," she moaned.

"I know," I said, placing my hand on the floor between the two of us. "I got really mad today, too. I was trying to make a letter work on the word processor. I messed it up and didn't have any more paper. I got so upset. It's hard when you can't get things to be the way you want them."

While I talked, she took my hand and pulled it closer to her. Then she got up, still holding my hand. She began to look at the closet again.

"I wonder. Do you think one of those boxes might do?" I said, looking at the two boxes that had caused such turmoil before.

"That one I think we could use. And the picture would just curl a little right here," she said tentatively as she pressed her picture gently into the box.

"Yeah," I agreed. "I think if we work carefully that picture will just fit in there."

In a few minutes Alicia was slowly returning to the civilized world. As children often do after surmounting a terrifying emotion in this way, she seemed just a little more mature than before.

23. *Do No Harm*

There are parental behaviors that are undeniably harmful to children.

" "Be always sure you're right. Then go ahead." That was the instruction of the famous explorer and pioneer, Daniel Boone.

I wish parenting was so easy. Sometimes I'm just not sure whether I'm doing the right thing or not. Hindsight will surely tell me whether I was on track—but I yearn to know now.

One thing I can do for my children which I can be sure will be right. I can avoid harming them.

An ethical imperative that every physician learns in medical school is "Do No Harm." The principle is based on the notion that in dealing with something as complex as the human body, one may not be sure that every treatment will be helpful. But one should avoid knowingly harming or injuring a patient.

In the old days, some physicians engaged in bloodletting, a practice that was thought to cure a variety of ills. The practice probably hastened the deaths of countless people, some of whom might have survived without such treatment. At the time no one knew bloodletting was harmful. Now we know better.

This "do no harm" principle should be applied to child-rearing as well. There are things parents do that will harm their children. They must learn not to do them.

Let's be blunt. I'm not speaking of things that could cause harm. These things do cause harm. If you do them, your children will suffer. Parents who do these things aren't found in any particular social strata or economic background. They may be economically or professionally successful. They will usually tell you they love their children. They may be devout Christians. Other people may see them as pillars of the community. In fact, the more "normal" they seem, the more harmful these people may be to their children.

There are a number of parental behaviors that are undeniably harmful to children. Sexual abuse is one of them.

During the course of his or her career, the typical therapist will see countless people, mostly women, who were sexually abused as children. Over time, these therapists will learn to recognize the subtle, subjective signs of abuse these people display even before they openly reveal the truth about their pasts.

Though these signs cannot here be fully described, they illustrate the deep injury which sexual abuse inevitably causes the child. Often you see it in the eyes—a distant, vacant quality, as if a portion of the soul has been assaulted. Sometimes you hear it in their words. Other times their behavior gives them away. It's a presentation that says, "I've been used. I've been injured to my core."

When you've been sexually abused, not just your psychological skin has been cut. You've been sliced to the depths of your soul. There are scars which have never truly healed, even years later.

Sandy was middle-aged, divorced, and had four children. She seemed quiet, unassuming, self-effacing—nice, but hard to get to know. She looked tired, haggard, and burned out. She seemed fragile, almost too fragile to be a parent. She never seemed to have the strength to deal with her rowdy and difficult children.

Various physicians and counselors had seen Sandy. They diagnosed her as having a dysthmic disorder—a kind of depression that is chronic and simmers in the background, often throughout a person's life. They might even have assumed she had an inherited predisposition toward depression, so constant and unchanging was her mood.

But there was more to Sandy's story. She had never revealed that her father had often molested her when she was a small child.

Now at middle-age, far removed by years and miles from the one who had done this to her, she still had nightmares about the things done to her and the things her father said he would do if she ever told anyone. She still felt an intense guilt that perhaps there was something evil about her if her own father would want to do these terrible things to her. A closet writer, she had never dared show anyone one set of her poems filled with the darkness and helplessness of her early life.

Abuse harms children. It may be sexual as in Sandy's case, or it may be physical. Spankings that leave bruises are abuse. Hitting children in the face, throwing them against walls, beating them—these *are* abuse.

Children can be abused mentally. They can be teased unmercifully. I'm not talking about the kind of teasing that everyone, including the child, can laugh about. I'm talking about teasing that's done at their expense. Parents can hurt children by threatening to abandon them or withdraw their love.

Four-year-old Lana spilled her milk. Her mother, in a fit of rage, told Laura she had had enough and was leaving. Still screaming and yelling, her mother threw clothes in a suitcase, put on her coat, and walked out the front door, telling Lana she'd never be back.

Terrified, Lana watched her mother drive down the street. She believed she would never see her mother again. Ten minutes later her mother was back, unpacking her suitcase and telling Lana she hoped she'd "learned her lesson" and would be a better child.

Some parents play catch-22 with their children. They place their children in dilemmas the children can't resolve. I remember a small boy I saw riding a mechanical horse outside the grocery store. It was a typical scene—except for the boy's response. Seated atop the moving horse with circus music playing, the lad was bawling his eyes out.

In a nearby parking space, his father sat in the family car exhorting him to get off the horse and in the car. Gunning the car's engine to emphasize his point, the father threatened to drive away if the boy didn't come right then. The child was faced with a no-win situation. He obviously feared falling to the pavement if he tried to get off the horse by himself. But if he didn't get off the horse right away, his father would punish him or even worse, leave him behind. So there the boy sat, sobbing away, paralyzed with fear. Putting children in psychological binds from which they can't recover is another form of mental abuse.

Children of alcoholics and drug users are also living in harm. Even if they aren't physically abused, as sometimes happens, there is a strange kind of neglect that occurs in alcoholic families. It's the experience of living with parents who may look like adults but don't act responsibly because chemicals have clouded their minds. These parents are erratic, unpredictable, or just plain out of it.

I worry about the harm some children experience. I worry as well about the parents of these children, because most are largely unconscious of what they are doing to their children.

Even those who are conscious of what they are doing mistakenly believe they can still control their behavior. "Next time" they will do better. Unfortunately, next time never comes. Other parents ease their guilt by rationalizing that their children bring the abuse on themselves.

You may be reading this chapter and feel uncomfortable right now because you know you are harming your child. If you're one of these people, there *is* hope for you.

The first thing you must do is admit you don't have the power to stop hurting your children on your own. Hurting children is a habit or pattern that builds up over time. It may have started with you being abused by your own parents when you were a child.

The second thing you have to do is to turn your life over to God. This is not a trite platitude. It is a recognition that if you are truly powerless to control your behavior, then you must seek the help of someone greater than yourself. It implies that you will trust God, put yourself in his hands, and open yourself to his help.

Then you must get professional help. "Pulling yourself up by your own bootstraps" won't work here. Almost no one gets better without outside help.

Perhaps a local mental health association can help you with a referral. Any professional you choose should meet two qualifications. He or she should be a certified or licensed mental health professional and should have experience working with the kind of problem you have. If you aren't sure, ask. Any competent professional will share information about her or his background.

Whatever you do, get help. Don't wait. The well-being of future generations will depend on the action you take.

24. When the Problems Get Complex . . .

Problem solving takes time, but it's worth it.

Todd is a curly-headed second-grader with a penchant for soccer and blue jean jackets. Sometimes he likes to join the other boys in chasing the girls around the playground at recess. But mostly he's a remarkably compassionate and caring child.

It's the second semester of the school year. Until now Todd's parents, Steve and Judy, have heard nothing but good news from the school about Todd. Each report card has used adjectives like well-mannered and studious.

One night in March the phone rings and Steve answers. It's Mrs. Hertz, Todd's teacher. She asks if Steve and Judy can come to a conference to discuss Todd. "It's nothing major," she says, "but something's changed in Todd's behavior."

At the conference, Mrs. Hertz says that Todd seems to be wanting more and more of her time; he becomes frustrated if she can't or won't give it.

The other day, Mrs. Hertz notes, the children were in the midst of a new assignment and Todd asked her for help. She told him she would help just as soon as she finished with several other children. Next thing she knew, Todd was in the back of the room, collapsed on the floor, pouting. Two days before, Todd and another boy had been sent to the counselor due to a squabble on the playground.

As Mrs. Hertz speaks, Steve and Judy suddenly realize that some gradual but significant changes have been taking place at home too. Todd has become a bear when he gets home from school. He's cranky as soon as he walks in the door. He balks when Judy tells him to do his schoolwork. He's especially resistant to doing his spelling, his most difficult and frustrating subject.

The other evening, after repeatedly refusing to do his work, and whining and complaining about his parents efforts to help him, Todd got a spanking. After the spanking, Steve noticed Todd curled up in the corner of the living room floor in a fetal position, thumb in his mouth. The event was dramatic because Todd had not done anything like that since he was a toddler.

After Steve and Judy tell Mrs. Hertz what has been going on at home, Mrs. Hertz wonders if Todd is getting enough affirmation. She gives the couple several articles to read on how to build children's self-esteem and self-confidence.

Steve and Judy read the articles and decide that, as an experiment, they will try a number of the suggestions for a week, then reevaluate Todd's behavior. They work hard to affirm Todd and watch for opportunities to encourage him when he's on track. At the end of the week, Todd has made minimal improvement. Judy calls the teacher and there's been little change at school either.

Steve and Judy are at a crossroad. Some parents become exasperated at this point and throw up their hands or lower the boom.

Steve and Judy put their heads together. As they think things over, they both have a sense that self-esteem isn't the real issue. After all, they have prided themselves on giving their children lots of affirmation. They wonder if the problem is more complex than they first imagined. They know complex problems demand good problem-solving strategies.

A good problem-solving strategy requires the following:

1. An understanding of what the problem is.
2. An investigation of all background issues that might help you understand why the problem exists.
3. The use of creative thinking to come up with possible solutions to the problem.
4. The implementation of the best of these solutions.
5. A way of evaluating whether the solution worked.

When self-esteem building doesn't help, Steve and Judy have a meeting one night after the children go to bed. They take out pencil and paper and write down their best understanding of the problems. They base their list on things they know have happened—things Todd is actually doing. This is what they write.

1. Todd wants more attention at school and becomes openly frustrated when he doesn't get it.
2. Todd is more irritable and easily frustrated at home after school.
3. Todd has more disagreements with his friends at school.
4. Todd's most difficult subject in school is spelling.

After examining the list, they look for background issues that may underlie the problems. Why, Steve wants to know, does Todd seems to want more attention in school than he did earlier in the school year? What could be happening at home that would encourage him to be more irritable there? Who are Todd's friends? What kinds of interaction is he having with them?

Steve and Judy start their investigation by observing everything that might give clues. Judy purposely volunteers to assist with an activity in the classroom so she can observe Todd there. Steve and Judy review the notes from their meeting with Mrs. Hertz. They observe Todd's behavior and their own after he comes home from school.

Then they list everything they've been able to learn that might conceivably be related to the problem. Here's what they find.

1. Judy notices that in the past two months, Todd has become best friends with two boys in his class. Both pout openly and with gusto when they don't get what they want. In her school observation, Judy notices one of the boys using this method to encourage Todd to play only with him and not be involved with the other boys. She realizes that some of the behavior she has seen in Todd at home looks amazingly like the pouty behavior displayed by the two boys.
2. Steve and Judy admit that as Todd's after-school behavior has deteriorated, they have allowed him more rather than less latitude. Todd would normally come home, have a snack, then begin his homework. But it became so frustrating to deal with his resistance to doing his homework that Steve and Judy began putting off telling him to do it. To be sure, they had tried to punish him too, but that wasn't leading to an improvement in Todd's behavior.
3. Judy notices in her classroom observation that Todd's attention-seeking behavior increases whenever the class is working on spelling.

Steve and Judy sit down late one night to discuss their findings and hammer out creative solutions. They start with the things they can work on themselves. They believe Todd needs more, rather than less, structure after school. But they know they must come up with a way to do this that will encourage rather than discourage Todd.

They make a big chart using colored markers to show Todd what is expected in the afternoons after school. The chart looks something like this:

AFTER SCHOOL SUCCESS CHART
PROGRAM

1. Eat snack.
2. Do homework and clean up room as soon as you finish snack.
3. After all homework is done and your room is clean, you may have FREE PLAY until supper.

STEP DISCIPLINE PLAN

Step 1. One warning to follow program.
Step 2. Go to Time Out Chair to settle down and prepare to do work.
Step 3. Spanking.

Steve explains the chart to Todd over the weekend when things are relatively quiet. He tells him they'll follow this program every day. Steve stresses that when Todd does his work he will be allowed free play with his friends. Steve also goes over the step discipline plan which they will apply one step at a time if Todd chooses not to comply with the Success Chart. Though Todd doesn't say much, Steve can sense he likes the chart.

To help Todd with his spelling, they include extra spelling practice as a part of homework each day, using words Todd is trying to master. They mix easy words with hard words. They dictate the words as if they're master of ceremonies for a spelling game show on TV. And they celebrate whenever Todd spells a word correctly.

Steve and Judy meet again with Mrs. Hertz. They make sure to be positive and express appreciation to her for not giving in to Todd's pouting. They speak with her briefly about their concerns that Todd seems to be "copying" some of his pouty behavior from his two friends.

The next week, Mrs. Hertz changes the seating arrangement in the class so Todd can interact with other boys in addition to the troublesome boys. Steve and Judy also encourage some new peer relationships by allowing Todd to invite several other boys over to his house to play.

Two weeks later Steve and Judy evaluate again. They call Mrs. Hertz to get her perspective. All agree that Todd's behavior and outlook both at school and at home have improved. There are still isolated episodes of Todd pouting but these are far fewer than before. Mrs. Hertz is happy that her "old Todd" is back. Steve and Judy found that the positive steps on their Success Chart worked so well, they never had to resort to spanking.

Some problems in parenting defy easy solution. A problem-solving strategy is needed to solve them. The parents must assess these kinds of situations thoroughly to understand what the problem is. The idea here is not to play armchair psychologist. Leave that to the professional. Instead, see yourself as a detective investigating the observable causes of your child's behavior. You are looking for cause-effect relationships—what is the cause A that is leading to behavior B in your child?

Once you know the cause you can develop and apply some creative solutions to change the cause-effect relationships for the better. You can then evaluate the success of your solutions to determine if you should do more or if indeed a professional needs to be consulted.

Problem solving is challenging. It takes time. But it's worth it, especially when you see a problem dissolve and you know you played a major part in the solution.

25. *Silver-Spoon Children*

Very young children don't need to be satiated. . . .

Harry and Sheilah just took their kids to a megaland theme park for summer vacation. They rode all the rides and saw all the sights. They also spent lots of time at refreshment counters and souvenir shops. Sure, most people visit the culinary and curio islands when they go to a theme park.

It's just that between most every ride, Harry was buying the kids either a soft drink, an ice cream, a "shine-in-the-dark" bracelet, or one of those drop-'em-in water colored rocks that grow. Harry is not a rich man. But by noon, the kids were so stuffed with junk food they could hardly move. And Sheilah had to rent a locker to put all the loot in.

Harry and Sheilah's children were satiated. And it wasn't only on vacation. At Christmas, their living room was filled with so many toys that visiting relatives dubbed the place Toys 'R Harry.

Many kids may not be overwhelmed with goodies the way Harry's children are. But many of our kids grow up with "silver spoons" in their mouths. While children in the third world wonder if they will eat at all, our kids wonder only if they will have the Sugar Smacks or Fruit Loops.

Don't get me wrong. Having nice things is nice. But Harry's gush of goodies can do more harm than good, for several reasons.

First, satiation implies a kind of glutting, the satisfaction of an urge that's so complete it leaves a bad taste in your mouth. It's like eating one too many bowls of homemade ice cream or that extra piece of grandma's chocolate cake.

Chronically satiated children sometimes develop a slow, subtle, but growing disappointment with life. What do you do when you've done it all? What do you do after the ultimate video game has been played, the best sweet has been tasted, and the ultimate theme park conquered? Like the words of the Peggy Lee song, you ask, with increasing despair, "Is that all there is?"

Very young children don't need to be satiated because they are simply overwhelmed when we bombard them with a barrage of stimuli. They gain more from simple activities in line with their level of experience.

After we went to one of those big theme parks, I asked my four-year-old which three rides she liked best. Her response shocked me. One of the "rides" she enjoyed most was not on the official list of park attractions at all. It was the tram that takes visitors from the parking lot to the theme park entrance! So much for the monster coaster, the fun house, and the hall of mirrors.

Simple activities stimulate rather than overwhelm young children. A simple jigsaw puzzle, watching a new bug on the back porch, or dressing up in big people clothes are plenty for most little ones. "Children's museums," popular in many towns throughout America, are good examples of places that provide young children with the opportunity to be stimulated by everyday things.

Some children who have it all become instant gratification junkies, constantly in search of their next "fix." They don't have time to wait, to be patient, because they're rushing headlong toward the next peak experience. These children tend to be impulsive. They can't delay gratification. They can't put off pleasure now for pleasure in the future. They can't because they have seldom had the opportunity.

I realize some children have trouble delaying gratification because they suffer from hyperactivity or a learning disorder. I'm not talking about these children. I'm referring to children who have been given so many unrestricted goodies that they come to expect this prosperity. These children become intensely frustrated when they can't have what they want.

Blessing children with everything can be a curse in disguise. Everybody needs to learn how to tolerate frustration because life is frustrating. Ultimately there is no "sugar daddy" who can change reality. You can't always get what you want.

What's more, we need to teach children to delay gratification because some rewards in life can't be achieved without it. You can't get a high school diploma without delaying gratification for 12 years. Physicians don't put an M.D. behind their name without years of study and years more to obtain a license. Most good marriages take years before they really solidify. Couples have to work through and deal with many conflicts before lasting intimacy develops.

Children don't suddenly gain the patience, fortitude, and foresight to tackle such challenges out of the blue. They can tolerate them only if they have had the opportunity to take on smaller hurdles early in life. While many parents could, with money, erase some of their children's obstacles, they shouldn't.

You could take junior down to the store tomorrow and buy him a bicycle. But why not encourage him to earn some of the money toward its purchase? He'll appreciate the bicycle a lot more, he'll feel proud that he was mature enough to have a part in its purchase, and he'll learn something about the value of things. By "programming" a hurdle for your child, you help him learn some valuable lessons for later.

Psychologists today are seeing many people who have come to be referred to as transitional adults. These are young adults having difficulty making the adjustment from the dependency of childhood to the independence of adulthood. Many are perpetual college students. Some have finished college but have gone back home to live with mom and dad. Some never left home in the first place. They may avoid employment and have little inclination to understand things like the need for income, health insurance, pensions, and the like.

Some of these people are like this because no one ever programmed hurdles for them. No one set reasonable challenges for them to overcome so they could gain the self-confidence to face the real world with at least the minimum amount of courage and persistence needed to succeed.

Note that I said no one ever set *reasonable* challenges for them. The best programmed hurdles are reasonable. They are set with forethought and in such a way that, with some effort, the child can hope to master them. Obviously the parent who programs impossible hurdles will only discourage the child's quest to learn to work toward goals despite frustration.

Programming surmountable hurdles fosters creativity, too. Children who are given reasonable challenges are encouraged to use their own creative powers to make things happen. They learn not to wait passively for happiness to come to them.

Recently I stopped in at a small country store while on a trip to the hills. It was the kind of place where the old folks sit outside on tree stumps chatting, and the checkers still have to ring up your purchases rather than scan them. There were no video games to play. There was seemingly little of interest there for a small child, save pink rubber balls on sale and the usual candy and cookies.

As I walked toward the back of the store to find a box of kitchen matches, I heard a recurrent plopping noise coming from the next aisle. Quietly I peeped around the corner. There, in the middle of the aisle, was a young girl holding one of the store's toilet plungers in midair. She was aiming it toward an imaginary target on the linoleum floor. Having sighted her target, she dropped the plunger and laughed as it plopped and stuck to the floor. Then tugging hard, she disengaged it and began looking for another target on the floor to aim for.

This girl didn't need a video arcade. Had there been one, it might have kept her from using her own creative powers. All she really needed was a little challenge—an old country store, a plunger, and a little imagination.

26. What Do You Do with an Angry Child?

Be angry but do not sin.

—Paul, the apostle (Eph. 4:26)

Our four-year-old got very angry with my wife one day. It seems Bette wouldn't allow her to go outside when *she* wanted to go outside. It had already been a long day, one of those days when your child exited the bed on the wrong side and she and you never fully recovered!

It happened right after my wife said "no" for the last time. Our darling daughter's face turned beet red. Suddenly she let loose a barrage of rage and threats that went something like this.

"Why you say that? You *always* say that. You make me so mad, and I gonna spank you bad, and I gonna put you in a trash, and I gonna throw you outside!"

Bette asked, "You're going to throw me in the trash?"

Our daughter turned to the side in disgust. Looking at Bette out of the corner of her eye, she said "You know I just talkin' Momma!"

For most parents I know, dealing with their children's anger is like trying to swallow a tablespoon of peanut butter without milk. It doesn't go down well.

The main problem is that parents nowadays aren't sure how to react to an angry child. Some aren't even sure children should be allowed to get angry. These parents were brought up with "children should be seen and not heard." They find it hard to listen to a child raise his voice.

Others have been influenced by a permissive posture that encourages parents to let their children experience anger, perhaps even act it out if necessary. Anger is like a pressure valve, so the theory goes. If children express it freely, it will not build up until the child explodes.

Most parents, influenced by both theories, are paralyzed. In their ambivalence, these parents never develop a consistent plan for dealing with their child's anger. Some days they react to their child's temper by tightening the parental screws.

Other days they allow the floodgates to open and watch the anger roll out. They watch it roll out, that is, until they come to the end of their patience. At that point, Junior usually gets a lesson in "There's no fury like that of a parent trod on once too often by an irritable child."

I have a plan for dealing with my children's anger. It's based on several assumptions.

There is nothing inherently bad about anger. Anger is an emotion, a feeling that is a response to stress. It is partly physiological and partly psychological. It is common to all human beings, though undoubtedly some people show their anger more directly than others. Anger in some form is not optional. Like sleeping and eating, it is a natural part of human behavior. Anger will be a part of my child's life whether I want it to be or not.

The problem with anger is the way it is expressed. The apostle Paul said, "Be angry but do not sin; do not let the sun go down on your anger" (Eph. 4:26, RSV). It is not wrong to be angry. Some ways of expressing anger are wrong. Letting anger fester into resentment (letting the sun go down on your anger) or abusing someone else, whether physically or emotionally, is wrong.

Anger can be expressed appropriately. Anger can be channeled for constructive purposes. I can use it to warn others that I am incensed by their behavior, to help them understand how I feel, and to communicate openly with them. Anger is a source of motivation. I can let it motivate me toward a destructive course. But I can also let it motivate me in constructive directions, as when I use it to energize me toward meeting good goals.

Having started with the assumption that anger in and of itself is not bad, I want specific standards that will help me guide my children toward constructive dealing with their anger. I want them eventually to learn a method for dealing with anger that will serve them well when they become adults. I've come up with the following general rules.

1. I will not allow my children to hit, bite, scratch, or otherwise physically act out against me or other people. These behaviors aren't appropriate for adults *or* for children.

I will stop these behaviors when they occur and remove my child from the situation. I will apply discipline appropriate to the age of the child and the situation.

2. I will teach my children that destroying property is not an effective way of dealing with anger. I will stop them from destroying things whenever I can. When they do destroy things, I'll teach them that doing so always has natural consequences.

3. I will allow my children verbal expression of their anger, even toward me. I want them to learn good ways to verbalize their anger. Here are some good ways to say it:

I'm mad at you!
I'm angry with you!
When *[some event]* happens, I get so mad.
I'm mad at what you did. I want you to do *[alternative behavior]* instead.

4. Temper tantrums aren't acceptable. People who consistently

have tantrums as children learn to be pouters and bellyachers as adults. I'll stop temper tantrums by not encouraging them. Temper tantrums exist only where there is an audience. When my child has a temper tantrum I'll make sure she doesn't hurt herself. But I'll act quickly either to remove the child from my presence or remove myself from the child's presence.

5. As my children get older and more verbal, they'll want to argue with me more. I want my children to have an opinion and know ways to express it. I want them to know that their opinions do affect my thinking and that I do want to hear how they feel. I also want them to know, however, that as the parent I am the final authority.

At our house, I'll help my children learn how to express themselves appropriately. But I'll also encourage them to stop themselves from carrying on a discussion or argument beyond the point where it is constructive for either one of us.

6. I'll allow my children to express their anger a bit more candidly at home than in public. The reality of human relationships is that we expect more anger expression at home than in public.

7. Perhaps most important, I want to teach my children that they can control their anger. Children need to *believe* that they control their anger.

Bernie grew up watching his father throw chairs through windows and shove tables across the room every time he went into a rage. Bernie tried not to do this himself, but sometimes he did. If you asked why, he'd tell you that when the going got really tough, he didn't really believe he could control his temper.

From the time they are toddlers, you can begin teaching your children that they can control their anger. If one flies into a rage and you have to take him bodily to a time-out room, tell him he can sit in this room until he settles down. Then he can come talk to you. Without saying so directly, you've suggested to him that if he has time-out, he *will* calm down. He *will* be able to return and be a meaningful part of family interaction.

If a young toddler gets totally and physically out of control, you might sit down and hold her in a bear hug, gently limiting her from flailing around. As you hold her, you can tell her you will help her learn to calm down.

Your children also need to see you control your anger so they'll know how to control theirs. They'll watch you cool down before you deal with anger. They'll see you try to deal with your anger by trying to change the situation that made you angry if you can find a way to do so. They'll see you distract yourself from the frustrations you can do nothing about.

The secret to success with anger is to learn to express it appropriately and channel it constructively. Most of us could learn to deal with our anger more effectively. Your children need to learn to get the emotion out without hurting anybody. Then they need to work out the situation they're angry about. Sometimes that means dealing with another person. Sometimes it will mean dealing with themselves.

27. "Mommy, Daddy . . . I'm Scared!"

The first thing a child wants when he's afraid is for someone to recognize and validate his feelings. . . .

It's late one night. Dad sits alone in the living room, looking through the newspaper. He senses a presence nearby. He glances up. There in the doorway is his three-year-old, standing quietly, meekly staring at him. He's clutching a small pillow to his head, which is cocked to one side. In the faint light, a tear is visible, glistening on his rounded cheek.

"Daddy . . . I'm scared," he says, a tremble in his voice.

Young children experience fears, anxieties, and worries just as adults do. The content of their fears may be different from ours. They may "see" monsters in the shadows of their room late at night. They may become terrified of the clowns at the circus. But their worries are no less real to them.

Children can also be bothered by the kinds of things that bother adults. I'll never forget an early anxiety-filled day. It came as a result of a trauma episode I witnessed. I was probably four or five.

It was a Saturday afternoon and I was riding back from the

hardware store with my dad. We came on an accident scene. There were people milling about and wrecked cars, and lots of glass. As I stared out my window, my eyes fixed on a passenger sitting upright in one of the wrecked cars. He seemed to be staring straight at me, though now I realize he was in shock and his eyes were glazed over. Lines of blood crisscrossed his face like a jigsaw puzzle, giving his face a broken, shattered appearance. I recoiled from the car window and turned my face, hoping to erase the horrid image from the screen inside my head. I couldn't.

For the rest of the afternoon, I kept seeing that man's face no matter where I was or what I did. As night began to fall my fear increased; I began to imagine that in the dark the man's broken, bloodied face was outside my window. I closed the blinds and shades but nothing seemed to help, because of course it was in my mind that the man's image was most clearly fixed.

Childhood fears and anxieties can be caused by many things. Children can be traumatized by some event as I was. They may be provoked to anxiety by one of the thousands of passing thoughts or worries that snake through a person's mind during the course of the day. The very young child may become frightened because of his limited experiences with people or things. He sees a circus clown for the first time and misjudges the unusual looking fellow to be foe rather than friend.

Some children are anxious because they have anxious parents. These children have either learned to be anxious by observing their parents' example, have inherited a biological predisposition toward anxiety, or both. No one knows how much is learned and how much is inherited. But in many cases we might guess that both factors are involved.

Many children go through a period of anxiety when their families are under some intense stress or change. A move to a different house, a change in jobs by one or both parents, a transfer to a new school, a death or illness in the family, difficulty in the parents' marriage—all may trigger anxiety in the child. Sometimes it's as if the child's display of anxiety is a barometer of the degree of stress rippling through the entire family.

Whatever the cause of the anxiety, we parents should always avoid criticizing children's fears. It would have done no good for someone to tell me that my fears of the man in the auto accident were stupid or silly or crazy.

In fact, discounting the objects of children's worries may actually cause children to hold on to the worry more fiercely. A parent will tell his child it's dumb to believe injured men's faces show up in the bedroom window glass. Technically, of course, he is right. But even if there is no real basis for the child's fear, the fear is real. That reality is what must be recognized and dealt with. The first thing a child wants when he's afraid is for someone to recognize and validate his feelings. He wants someone to say, "Seeing that face today must have scared you," or "I can understand that you're feeling shook up about what happened."

Children need parents who validate the reality of their fearful feelings even if the object of the fear is not real. What they don't need are parents who take their worries as an opportunity to go into hysterics themselves.

When Marissa was four, her mother got sick and had to be in the hospital for a week. When Mom came home she realized that in her absence Marissa had taken to pulling little pieces of her hair out. This is something children occasionally do when they are feeling an intense stress, such as having a mother hospitalized.

Marissa's mother was horrified and didn't hesitate to let Marissa know. The first time she caught her doing it, Mom's eyes got wide and she cried out, "What on earth do you think you're doing?" in a voice that would have been appropriate if Marissa had just pushed the button launching a nuclear warhead.

After the initial shock, Mom took the clinical approach and told Marissa this was "self-destructive behavior." Marissa might end up in a mental hospital some day if she kept this up. Marissa didn't know exactly what a mental hospital was, but from her mother's tone she could tell it wasn't Tiny Tim's Playland.

When nothing else worked, Mom turned to punishment. She

threatened Marissa with spanking if she didn't stop. The result? Marissa now worried not just about her mother's health and the possibility of losing her. She also worried about her hair pulling, and about the possibility of punishment. Consequently, she started pulling her hair more, sneaking around to do it to avoid detection and the anticipated spanking.

Parental worry about child worry convinces the child her anxieties are so powerful that now even the adults are overwhelmed by them. Faced with parents seemingly impotent in the face of her childhood fears, she worries even more.

When children worry, they need parents who will step beyond their own fears and offer them love and support mixed with a dose of problem-solving and confidence-building. The parent must convey by words, thoughts, and behavior the message, "I know this is scary for you, and I know that, in time, you will be able to overcome it, and I'll be around to help you."

This message communicates three things. It validates the child's fear as a real emotion worthy of attention. It implies that the child has the power within herself to defeat the fear. This is important because all of us must find our own ways to win over fear. Our parents won't always be around to help us. Finally, the message encourages the child that the parents will help her make it through the fright.

While conveying that message, we parents also need to be looking around for any sources of stress that aren't already obvious. Has there been a recent move? Has school just started? Is there conflict between the child and a friend? What's going on at home? Is Dad having trouble at work? Is one parent an alcoholic? Has a single mom started dating again? Is there conflict in the marriage? These are just a few of the issues that can increase stress to a flash point. Once they know the source of the stress, parents can work together with each other, the child, and perhaps other family members to deal with any stressors that can be changed.

Rod and Vicki sought marriage counseling when evidence accumulated that their child's nail biting was related to conflict in their marriage. Their clue came when their child asked if they were getting a divorce—something never thought of or mentioned.

Most childhood fears just need an understanding and comforting adult who can help the child find her own methods for calming the fear. One method we like to use is called visual imagery. Sometimes we call it "watching the 'movie' in our minds."

It's especially nice to use at bedtime. When one of the girls is a little nervous or frightened, we lie down on the bed with her and encourage her to close her eyes. We suggest that she imagine some pleasant and pretty place we've been to, such as a beach or a pleasant river in the hills. We encourage her to see all the pleasant things there. We might suggest she recall a time when she was lying down on the pew at church on Sunday, her head gently cradled in one of our laps, looking at the colors of the stained-glass, listening to the choir in the background, and singing about Jesus. Or we might have her picture a comforting Bible story.

When I worked at a pediatric hospital, the staff was often amazed at the scary and painful medical procedures children could tolerate using various types of visual imagery. In fact, children are often better at doing this than adults.

I don't remember exactly what my dad did for me the night I was traumatized by the shattered face in the window. I do know he was in the bathtub when I decided to come crying and knocking on the door for help. Parenting is never convenient! I imagine he said some comforting words, tucked me in, and perhaps stroked my head to help me calm down. Whatever he did, I relaxed and went to sleep. I woke next morning realizing, perhaps unconsciously, that anticipating the worst doesn't necessarily mean it will happen.

28. *What Does It Mean to Be Family?*

The family is the nucleus of civilization.

—Will and Ariel Durant

Over the past several decades, Dr. Nick Stinnett and his colleagues (Stinnett & DeFrain, 1985) have been studying strong families. They wanted to know what qualities strong families have in common which other families could emulate.

They collected data on thousands of families. Such studies always have some research flaws. But what is striking is that Stinnett and his colleagues consistently obtained the same results no matter how they evaluated the question. They used different sampling techniques. They studied different kinds of families—traditional, single-parent, and step-families. They evaluated minorities and families in other countries beside the U.S.

Time and again, in every study, across family types, they came up with the same themes. These suggested six basic characteristics of a strong family. These were

1. Commitment
2. Spending time together
3. Appreciation
4. Good communication patterns
5. High degree of religious orientation
6. Ability to deal with crises in a reasonable manner

Strong families need members who are *committed* to one another. They put family needs first even when it means sacrificing whatever would keep them from being an enriching part of the family. Our culture's ideals about commitment are stated well in the traditional wedding vows. Unfortunately real people often fall short of the vows, and the threats to commitment are more subtle than we often suppose.

One of the biggest threats is work. Dedication to work is a virtue, but like most virtues it has a dark side. Many fathers, and increasingly mothers, commit themselves with pure motives to the role of "provider," only to end up strangers to their own children. Other parents have followed the call to the mission field, the board room, or the city council, only to come home to families in shambles.

Perhaps the biggest danger in work is that you can immerse yourself in it so fully. Through work you can hide from your family's disintegration, often until too late to do anything about it.

Commitments to people outside the family can weaken the commitment within too. Perhaps none is as damaging as the affair. Affairs do affect children and families, even if family members don't know about them—and they *do* know about them more frequently than unfaithful spouses ever suppose!

It is impossible to have an affair and maintain the needed level of commitment to one's family. If for no other reason, there is the simple matter of time and energy. Time and energy expended on an affair is relational energy siphoned away from children and spouse. No one can serve two masters.

At the most fundamental level, commitment means *spending*

time together. Unfortunately more and more families do less and less of it these days. The family meal is often a barometer of the amount of time a family spends together. Nowadays families seldom share a common lunch, and probably not a common breakfast. In too many cases they don't even share dinner.

Spending time together doesn't mean spending every waking minute with each other. Families suffocate each other when they do that. Each member of the family needs outlets for individual fulfillment. But spending time together, and lots of it, is key.

When I surveyed my five-year-old and asked about her happiest memories in life, ten of her eleven memories were of family together things. Among others she mentioned were these:

1. Playing together outside
2. Going to Nana and Papa's
3. Going to Grandmother Schmidt's
4. When Jan and Jodi (cousins) spent the night
5. Going on walks with you guys
6. Sitting together in the recliner

Get the point? I did.

Families which *appreciate* one another find and recognize the unique contribution each person makes to the family unit. One child is quiet and reserved and talented in building puzzles, drawing pictures, or reading books. Another is expressive and never meets a stranger. She is a natural ambassador wherever the family goes.

Appreciation means seeing the special talent each person brings to the family unit. Most important, it means complimenting and expressing appreciation to that person.

Good communication patterns are important to strong families. Some families never talk. They walk around in silence as if thinking other family members could see their needs by reading their minds. Then they become sullen and prune-faced when their minds aren't read.

Other families are like volcanoes trying to coexist within 1,650 square feet of heated and cooled suburbia. They scream and yell at each other until the four walls bow out and flame shoots up the chimney. They ventilate lots of feeling but rarely get their problems solved.

Every family communicates. Whether in deft silence or screams that rock the neighborhood, we all communicate something. It's just that some families communicate in better ways than others. Good communication helps family members truly understand each other. Good communication may start with a conflict but it leads to a solution. Whether it is loud or soft, angry or happy, it builds the family up and pulls them closer together rather than farther apart.

Strong families have a *high degree of religious orientation.* That's an academic way of saying that the families in Stinnett's research consistently mentioned a unifying force in their lives that caused them to find purpose and meaning in life, transcend self, and care for others.

Thousands of years from now, archaeologists are likely to dig up remnants of a lost civilization: ours. They'll probably happen upon a street of tract homes while constructing some new supersonic subway system.

They'll find a row of houses relatively intact. In a central place in the corner of the main room of each habitat, they'll find a rectangular box with a screen! Some will have "rabbit ears" and some won't. Seeing names like Zenith and Quasar, they'll probably reason that these boxes were strange idols worshiped by a primitive culture.

Maybe that assessment won't be too far off. Sometimes it seems as though our ultimate concern is to make it through the day so we can collapse on the couch and receive our nightly sustenance from the electronic marvel called the television. The people in Stinnett's sample were talking about a power greater than that.

Christians have spiritual resources available to them that, when fully used, improve family life. Worshiping together at church, spontaneously singing a hymn together at home, or gathering in the living room to light the advent candles at Christmas are all spiritual activities which can bring us closer to our heavenly father. At the same time, they strengthen the bonds within the earthly family.

With God's help, we can continue to love other members of our family even when in conflict with them over their behavior. More than a sentimental love, this is a steadfast love that sees beyond the immediate conflict to the long-range covenant we've made. It helps us focus on solving conflict and thus allows us to grow in our ability to relate healthily to one another.

In our families, we seek to speak the truth to one another in love (Eph. 4:25, 15). When we get angry, we want to avoid denying our anger, but we want to deal with it in constructive ways (Eph. 4:26). Above all, we want to walk in love with one another just as Christ has loved us (Eph. 4:32; 5:2).

Strong families also have the ability to *deal with crises in a reasonable manner.* In part that can be a by-product of a faith which strengthens us to "bear one another's burdens" (Gal. 6:2). It also means learning the coping skills necessary to deal with life. Life isn't easy. Often it isn't fair. Getting through it demands that you take control of what you can, maintain the flexibility to roll with the punches, and keep a sense of humor throughout.

There were six attributes that depicted the strong family. Noticeably absent from the list were prominence, income level, physical attractiveness, or where the families lived. It is even conceivable that some of the absent attributes might conflict with being a strong family.

Often strong families are made up of regular people just trying to live good, decent lives. Maybe that's just as well, because it makes it all the more likely that most of us, with some guidance and practice, can build a healthy family.

29. He Wants Them to Fly!

Like an eagle that stirs up its nest, that hovers over its young, He spread His wings and caught them, He carried them on His pinions.

—Deut. 32:11, NASV

"All passengers please fasten your seat belts as we prepare to take off." As the stewardess began making her other announcements over the intercom, we buckled in for a family vacation flight. My seven-year-old sat next to me. She was too young to remember her only other airplane ride several years before. In the seats behind us, my wife and four-year-old looked out the window as the plane began to barrel down the runway.

The seven-year-old, pensive and excited, put her fingers in her mouth and started biting her nails. But as the plane rose and banked into the blue Texas sky, she let out a loud "Wheee!" Turning back to her younger sister she shouted, "Alicia, how do you *feel*?"

"I feel *fiiiine!*" Alicia yelled back. Her squeal of delight made the businessman in the three-piece suit on the next aisle stare at all of us over the top of his half-frame glasses. Then even he smiled.

Childhood—a wonderfully frightening time when you're always on the edge of adventure. Every day you're learning new things you've never seen or done before. Like a baby bird poised for flight at the edge of the nest, you hope to soar to the heights, but fear plummeting to the depths.

The edge of the nest where your child sits is defined not just by the limits of her knowledge, but also by her motor skills, abilities, and self-confidence. Take learning the piano. Even children who like the instrument often find themselves tested to the limit of their capacity each time they sit down to play. Eyes fixed intently on the practice page, hands to the keyboard, tongue wrapped tightly around the edge of an open mouth are all signs of the challenge.

You can usually tell when your child is living at her edge. She'll be extra sensitive, more concerned about what you think, and twice as likely to shift her mood in a moment's notice.

Our children desperately need our encouragement at these times. Their confidence and self-esteem are on the precipice. A kind word as they struggle through may make all the difference.

"Hey, I like the way that sounds," you might say when a piano piece is near its end. "I know that piece is really hard for you," said during a particularly difficult practice can let the child know you are behind her.

Sometimes children encounter obstacles they can't overcome, at least not in the conventional way. It could be they're being asked to do something beyond their stage of development. In that case, they need to be allowed time to develop.

At other times, they're being asked to do something not in line with their talents. In those cases, we must allow the child a chance to sidestep to an activity where she can use her own special skills successfully.

Almost every pediatric hospital has its stories about boys and girls brought to the hospital with stomach ulcers, headaches, or other painful physical problems. Usually these children have been through acres of medical tests. At some point, the psychologist is brought in for consultation—and discovers that the symptoms are at their worst when the little league season starts or the ballet recital is due.

Often, investigating further, the psychologist finds a parent who's pushing the child to become the next Mickey Mantle or Margot Fonteyn. Such children suddenly lose their symptoms and begin to blossom when their parents allow them to sidestep to an activity in line with the unique set of talents with which God has blessed them.

We parents can play a big part in supporting our children, whether encouraging them to take a risk, to wait until they grow a bit, or to sidestep to something that fits better.

We aren't alone in our desire that they do well. Throughout the Old Testament there is indication of God's care and concern for his Hebrew people. In poetic verse, God is seen carrying his people in flight, like an eagle carrying its young (Deut. 32:11). He provides the power for his people to fly above their limitations.

> but they who wait for the Lord shall renew their strength, they shall mount up with wings like eagles, they shall run and not be weary, they shall walk and not faint (Isa. 40:31, RSV).

I'm convinced that God, the author and facilitator of all life, wants the same thing for my children. He wants them to fly!

If that's true, my home is their launching pad. In the years my children are with me, it's my job to equip them for their trek through life. Part of my job is to infuse—to teach concepts, principles, and behaviors. It's also my job to provide enough freedom so that they become not a copy of me, but themselves—the people God created them to be.

A couple of summers ago we were at Mo-Ranch, a church camp near Kerrville, Texas. A big catwalk connects the two sections of the camp across a wide, deep arroyo. Though this footbridge is steel and sturdy enough, it vibrates as you walk across. If you look down, you can peer through the holes in the steel grid and see the ground far below.

As I walked across the bridge ahead of my family, I wondered how Joy would respond to it. Three years before, when we had visited the camp, she had started the week fearful of walking across the bridge. She would take a few sheepish steps, just enough to say she had ventured out. Each time I'd encourage her, but as quickly as she came forward, she would run back to the safety of solid ground.

As time went by, she grew bolder. One day she started venturing straight across the catwalk. As she reached me, she announced, "I'm not going to be afraid. I'm four now. When you're three, *then* you're afraid. But I'm four now." With that, she walked to the other side.

Now, three years later, I watched to see what she would do. She crossed without hesitation, as if the catwalk had never been a problem.

Life for children is a never ending series of challenges. Each carries its own excitement and terror. Once a challenge is met, children move to the next. As they move toward, over, and through their challenges, God gives us the enjoyable task of encouraging and assuring our children of their worth. God wants them to fly, and we get to cheer them on!

30. *Bless Me, Bless My Child*

Three months after Alicia was born, we brought her to church to dedicate her—and us—to the Lord. My wife and I struggled to find the words to express to our church and to God just how we felt about this baby and about our job as parents. We wanted to share our joy, our thanksgiving, and our neediness.

We borrowed from the Bible, we wrote out the rest, and all of it flowed naturally from our hearts. This is what we said, on behalf of ourselves and all parents struggling to describe the indescribable.

Glory to God in the highest and on earth, peace,
goodwill toward all.

Our souls exalt the Lord,
and our spirits rejoice in God, our Savior,
for he has had regard for us, his servants.

God, in your infinite wisdom, you have seen fit
to lend this baby to us. We give you thanks for
this great gift and we acknowledge that Alicia,
and all of us, belong to you.

We pray for wisdom,
    courage,
        creativity, and
        patience

as we seek to nourish Alicia toward
    spiritual,
        physical, and
        emotional
           maturity.

Help us to support and discipline her with balance and always in love.

And may this church family be a source of strength to her, teaching and equipping her to make her way into the large world.

       Amen

Select Bibliography

Ballard, S, N. and Fleck, J. R.
  1975 "The teaching of religious concepts: A three-stage model." *Journal of Psychology and Theology*, 3: 164-171.

Braga, J. and Braga, L.
  1976 *Children and Adults*. Englewood Cliffs: Prentice-Hall.

Durant, W. and Durant, A. Cited in Peter, L. J.
  1977 *Peter's Quotations*. New York: William Morrow.

Erikson, E.
  1963 *Childhood and Society*, 2nd ed. New York: Norton.

Fantz, R. L.
  1961 "The origin of form perception." *Scientific American*, 204: 66-72.

Foster, R. J.
  1985 *Money, Sex, and Power*. San Francisco: Harper & Row.

Grant, W. W.
  1983 *The Caring Father*. Nashville: Broadman.

Hart, B. M.; Reynolds, N. J.; Baer, D. M.; Brawley, E. R.; and Harris, F. R.
  1968 "Effects of contingent and noncontingent social reinforcement on the cooperative behavior of a preschool child." *Journal of Applied Behavioral Analysis*, 1: 73-76.

Joubert, J. Cited in Austin Heights Baptist Church Newsletter, September 1985

Krumboltz, J. D. and Krumboltz, H. B.
  1972 *Changing Children's Behavior*. Englewood Cliffs: Prentice-Hall.

Miller, K.
  1967 *A Second Touch*. Waco: Word Books.

O'Leary, K. D., and Schneider, M. R.
  Catch'em being good [Film]. Champaign, Ill.: Research Press.

Patri, A. Cited in Wallis, Charles L., ed.
  1965 *The Treasure Chest*. New York: Harper & Row.

Paynter, R.
  1983 *Newsletter of the Lake Shore Baptist Church*. Waco.

Rosenhan, D. and White, G. M.
  1967 "Observation and rehearsal as determinants of prosocial behavior."
  Journal of Personality and Social Psychology, 5: 424-431.

Rubin, R. R. and Fisher, J. J.
  1982 *Your Preschooler*. New York: Collier Books.

Sandburg, C. Cited in Wallis, Charles L., ed.
  1965 *The Treasure Chest*. New York: Harper & Row.

Stinnett, N. and DeFrain, J.
  1985 *Secrets of Strong Families*. Boston: Little, Brown, and Company.

Tournier, P.
  1967 *To Understand Each Other*. Richmond: John Knox Press.

Van Gogh, V.
  1978 *The Complete Letters of Vincent Van Gogh*. Boston: New York Graphic
  Society Books/Little, Brown, and Company.

The Author

Randolph K. Sanders is a clinical psychologist who practices in San Antonio and New Braunfels, Texas. Prior to coming to the San Antonio area, Sanders was executive director of the Samaritan Counseling Center of East Texas and an adjunct faculty member at Stephen F. Austin State University.

Sanders earned his Ph.D. at the Graduate School of Psychology, Fuller Theological Seminary (Pasadena, Calif.). He also has degrees from Baylor University (Tex.) and Stephen F. Austin State University (Tex.). He trained in a number of settings, including the Childrens Hospital of Los Angeles.

In addition to his clinical practice, Sanders provides seminars to churches and other organizations on topics such as parenting and stress. He writes articles for Christian magazines and has coauthored (with H. N. Malony) *Speak Up! Christian Assertiveness* (Westminster, 1985; Ballantine/Epiphany, 1986). He has been noted in *Who's Who in the South and Southwest*.

Sanders and his wife, Bette, have two children, Joy and Alicia. He and Bette serve as fourth-grade Sunday school teachers at their church, First Baptist in San Marcos, Texas. He enjoys camping, hiking, photography, and just being with his family. He was born in Houston, Texas.

For additional information on Dr. Sanders' seminars you may contact (512) 620-0869.